BUILDING

BUILDING
The Fight Against Gravity

MARIO SALVADORI

Drawings by Saralinda Hooker
and Christopher Ragus

A MARGARET K. McELDERRY BOOK

ATHENEUM   1979   NEW YORK

Library of Congress Cataloging in Publication Data
Salvadori, Mario George
Building: the fight against gravity.
"A Margaret K. McElderry book."
Includes index.
SUMMARY: An introduction to the basic principles of architecture and
engineering including a discussion of structural materials and their
properties and such problems as how skyscrapers are kept from swaying
excessively and buildings prevented from sinking into the ground.
1. Structures, Theory of—Juvenile literature. 2. Building materials—Juvenile
literature. [1. Structures, Theory of. 2. Building materials] I. Title.
TA634.S24   624'.17   79-14325
ISBN 0-689-50144-7

Published simultaneously in Canada by McCelland and Stewart, Ltd.
Manufactured by American Book/Stratford Press
Saddle Brook, New Jersey
Designed by Marjorie Zaum
First Edition

For
Niccolò
and
all my other young friends
who keep asking me
why buildings stand up

ACKNOWLEDGEMENTS

I wish to express my deep gratitude to the children of Harlem, who
joyfully started me on a new career
and
to Pearl Kaufman, who put the book together so many times with
love, patience and skill.

Contents

BUILDING

1

From Cave to Skyscraper

THIRTY THOUSAND YEARS AGO, MEN ROAMED FROM PLACE TO PLACE hunting animals for food and looking for wild plants to eat. As they were always moving, they did not build houses. They slept under the stars, got wet under the rain, sweated under the sun, and cooked their meals over open wood fires. Much later on, they began to put up shelters, tents made of animal skins, and tried to protect themselves from the weather. If they were lucky and roamed in mountainous areas, they might find caves where they could cook and sleep. Caves were better places to live in. But tents had the advantage of being easily moved. If the supply of animals or wild plants ran out, men could pull up stakes and set up housekeeping where there was more food. They literally "pulled up stakes" because they had found that, without ropes anchored to the ground, their tents could be blown away by the wind. So they fought the force of the wind and stiffened the tent by means of ropes attached to stakes driven into the ground (Fig. 1.1), just as we do today when we go camping.

Of course, for people to be able to live under the tent, a pole

1.1

made out of a tree branch had to support the top at the center, and the taller the pole, the taller the tent. It would have been comfortable to use poles tall enough to allow men to stand up under the tent, but it was not easy to do this.

If the pole were tall and thin it might bend and collapse under a high wind pressure or when the ropes were pulled too hard (Fig. 1.2). If the pole were thick, it would not collapse but would be heavy and hard to carry. The tent men had to be satisfied with thin, short sticks that were both light and stiff, so they could not stand up straight under their tents.

To make sure the wind would not pull out the stakes they also set heavy stones on the skin all around the bottom of the tent. The tent wouldn't blow away unless the wind could lift the weight of the stones and then pull out the stakes. The heavier the stones, the stronger the wind had to be to move them.

A few more thousands of years went by, and about ten thousand years ago men slowly began to learn a new way of getting food. Instead of eating wild plants, like rice that grew by itself in certain spots, they learned to plant vegetables, wheat, barley, millet and rye, to water them, to tend them, and to grow enough to feed their families without ever moving camp. At the same time men learned to catch wild animals and to feed and keep them in captivity. They domesticated dogs, asses, oxen, horses and turkeys and thus provided meat as well as vegetables and grain for themselves and their families without having to be on the move all the time. Mankind had discovered agriculture.

When early men had to break camp often and carry tents on their backs, they could not have very comfortable homes. But once they had found ways of staying in one place, they started to think

1.2

of building shelters that were larger, stronger and more comfortable than tents. As men learned to farm, they slowly became builders and their houses became larger and also taller.

Each family had its own permanent home. In cold climates it was usually made out of logs or stones set one on top of the other. In moderate climates it was built of mud mixed with straw, a material called *adobe*, while in hot climates it was made out of wood poles and thatched roofs (Fig. 1.3). When many families lived

1.3

near one another, their houses made up a village. In order to meet together and discuss common problems, the village people built large buildings that served both as their town halls and their churches (Fig. 1.4). To get from one house to another, they main-

1.4

tained well-kept paths, and, eventually, to go from village to village, they built roads. Since the roads often crossed deep rivers or rivers that flooded in the spring, bridges of tree trunks supported by wood poles had to be built (Fig. 1.5). When the roads had to cross

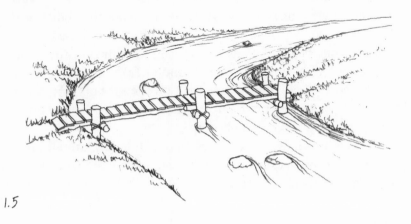

1.5

1.6

ravines in the mountains, suspension bridges with cables of vegetable-fiber rope and walking decks of wooden planks had to be strung across (Fig. 1.6). Gradually man learned how to use the materials he found in nature, like stone, wood, and vegetable fibers.

Some of these structures, like the pyramids of Egypt, which were built over four thousand years ago to house the bodies of the Pharaohs when they died, were as high as 482 feet and used millions of heavy stone blocks. Others, like the cliff dwellings of the Indians of Arizona and New Mexico, built around 1,000 A.D., had as many as four floors. These houses were built on the rims of cliffs to make it difficult for the enemy to attack them once the ladders used to climb into them had been pulled up.

Now, thousands of years later, man still builds himself houses; and although he does it often with man-made materials, like steel or bricks or concrete, he uses the same skills his ancestors did to fight the same natural forces and to make sure that his buildings will not fall down.

Modern man has learned to build high, but safely. There is a building in Chicago that is the tallest in the world. It is called the Sears Tower and is 1,454 feet tall. It has 110 floors, and yet it is perfectly safe (Fig. 1.7). Modern men have also learned to build

l.7

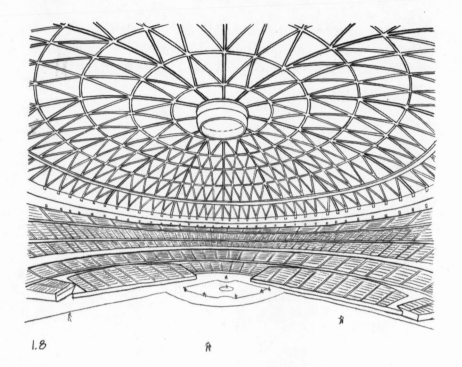

1.8

1.9

meeting halls, as their ancestors did, but they are so large that as many as 80,000 people can sit under the roof of one of them and watch a baseball or a football game (Fig. 1.8). Their suspension bridges are made out of steel and can cross rivers 8,000 feet wide, but they are built on the same construction principles used in the fiber-rope bridges made by their ancestors (Fig. 1.9).

This book will show you how tents and houses and stadiums and bridges are built and how you can build some lovely small models of these structures by using nothing but paper, strings, ice cream sticks or tongue depressors, glue and pins.

2
Building a Tent

THE PURPOSE OF THE TENT IS TO PROTECT US FROM THE WEATHER: to shade us from the sun, to prevent the rain or the snow from wetting us, and to stop the wind from blowing on us. The old tents were made of animal skins; modern tents are made of nylon fabric. To make our tent work we must keep the fabric up and spread out. But the fabric is so thin that it cannot stand on its own. We keep it up by using a stick or pole at the center of the tent. However, the pole cannot stand up by itself either, unless we push it deep into the ground, and if the ground is hard this may be difficult or impossible. So to keep the pole up we attach 3 or 4 ropes to its top and we anchor the ropes into the ground after pulling them taut. We can anchor the ropes either by tying their ends to stakes pushed into the ground in a circle some distance from the center pole, or by setting heavy stones on the ends of the ropes (Fig. 2.1). Then we can stretch the fabric over the ropes, pin it to the ropes, and we get a working tent.

Notice that the pole and the ropes and stakes have only one purpose: to keep the fabric up. They are the *structure* of the tent.

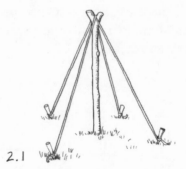

2.1

The purpose of a tent structure, like that of a building structure, is to make sure that the tent or the building will stand up. The purpose of the tent fabric, on the other hand, is to protect us: it makes the tent *function*. In a building, the thin outside walls and the roof protect us, they make the building function, but they must be kept up by vertical columns and horizontal beams of steel, concrete, or wood, which form the building *frame* or structure.

The outside walls and the roof of a building are often called its *skin* and the columns and beams its *skeleton*, since, as with the human body, the skin provides protection and the skeleton makes it stand up.

To build a model of a small tent you will need:

> a drinking straw for a center pole
> 4 thumb tacks or drawing pins
> a square slab of wood or Styrofoam. (A styrofoam slab 2 feet by 2 feet by one inch thick is most useful as a base to build models of structures. It can be bought for a few cents in a lumber yard or a hardware store, since slabs of Styrofoam are used for home insulation.)
> 2 pieces of string or thread, about 2 feet long or 3 times as long as the straw, for ropes
> paper
> glue

Cut 4 notches in one end of the straw about the same distance apart. Put the middle point of each piece of string into two opposite notches and anchor the ends of the strings to the square piece of wood or Styrofoam with the thumb tacks (Fig. 2.2).

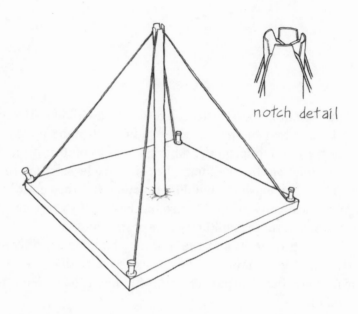

notch detail

2.2

To finish the tent model you must stretch a skin over the strings. The skin can be a handkerchief stapled to the strings, or 4 triangles of paper glued or stapled to the strings (Fig. 2.3). In one of the paper triangles a door flap can be cut and folded back.

The straw, once attached to the strings that are tacked down, stands up because to make it fall you would have to pull out the thumb tacks. We say that the straw is *stayed* by the strings, just as the pole in a real tent is stayed by the ropes and the stakes or stones. You will notice now that the *pull* on the strings *pushes down* on the straw. If you use a Styrofoam base, the straw actually makes a slight dent in the base.

In structures, if you pull on a rope or a string, we say that you

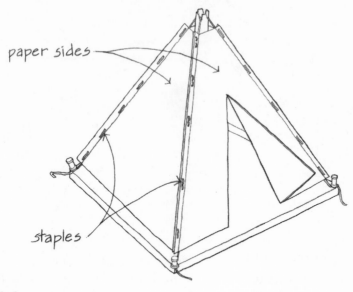

paper sides

staples

2.3

have put the rope or the string in *tension* or *tensed* it. If you push down on the pole or the straw from the top we say that the pole or straw is *compressed* or *in compression*.

To find out how it "feels" to be in tension, grab the knob of a closed door and pull on it: your arm is in tension. If you want to "feel" compression, push with your arm stretched against the door knob: your arm is in compression (Fig. 2.4). These two structural words, tension and compression, are most important. *All structures*, in a one-family house or a skyscraper, in an arch or a suspension bridge, in a large dome or a small flat roof, are *always* either in tension or in compression. Structures can only pull or push. If you understand how tension and compression work, you understand why structures stand up.

How do we recognize tension and compression? We cannot always put our arm where the structure is and "feel" these forces, but it is still quite easy to recognize them. Take a thin rubber band and pull it with your hands. You are putting the rubber band in

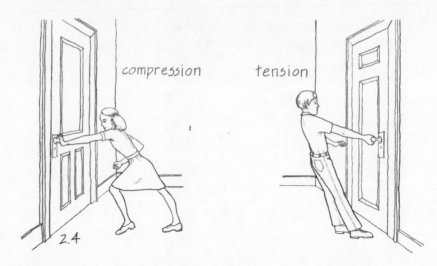

2.4

tension and the band becomes *longer* (Fig. 2.5a). You now know that whenever a part of a structure becomes longer it is in tension. Take a rubber sponge and push on it: the sponge becomes *shorter* in the direction in which you push. Whenever a part of a structure becomes shorter, it is in compression (Fig. 2.5b).

There is a catch to recognizing tension and compression simply by the lengthening and shortening of part of a structure, and you probably have noticed it already. The amount of lengthening and shortening in a structure is usually so small that it is not possible to see it with the naked eye. When you pulled on the strings of the tent model, the strings became longer, but only by a little bit. When you pushed on the top of the straw pole, the pole was shortened by only a little bit. (This is because the strings are stiffer than the rubber band and the straw is stiffer than the sponge.) Yet you could easily guess that the strings were in tension and the pole was in compression. If you imagine putting your arm where the structure is, most of the time you can guess how it would feel and whether it is in tension or compression.

Here are some examples.

The elevator in an apartment house hangs from steel cables. Imagine your arm as one of the cables and you will "feel" the tension on it caused by the weight of the elevator. The cables are slightly lengthened by this weight. They are in tension.

When you sit on a chair, your weight pushes down on the legs and makes them a little shorter. Imagine you are trying to hold up this weight with your arms and you will "feel" the compression. The pedestal that supports the Statue of Liberty works in the same way as the legs of a chair. The weight of the statue pushes on it and makes it a bit shorter.

A suspension bridge is also supported by steel cables, anchored on the ground, that go over the top of the bridge towers (see Fig. 1.9). The cables are in tension, like the strings staying your model of a tent. The bridge towers, like your straw tent pole, are in compression.

Imagine your arm stretched up as the trunk of a Christmas tree. The weight of the branches and of the trunk itself pushes down like your weight pushing down on the legs of a chair. The tree trunk is in compression.

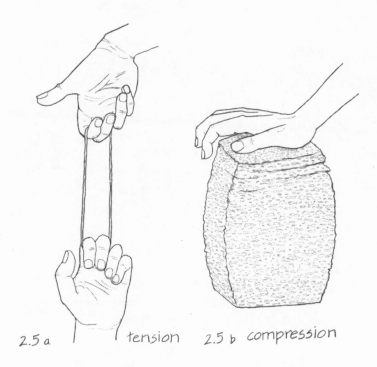

2.5 a   tension   2.5 b compression

If your arms were the stones of an arch bridge, they would be in compression. The weight of the stones themselves and the loads going over the bridge put the stones in compression.

If you are in any doubt about compression in an arch bridge, stand 2 feet away from a wall and lean on it, with your hands up against the wall and your body bent toward the wall (Fig. 2.6). You are now half an arch and you will feel the compression.

If you and one of your friends put your hands on each other's shoulders and move your feet away from each other, you will become a full arch and feel compressed by each other's weight (Fig. 2.7). But if your shoes slip on the floor and you begin to slide apart, the arch will collapse. Its ends must be firmly anchored to prevent it from spreading apart.

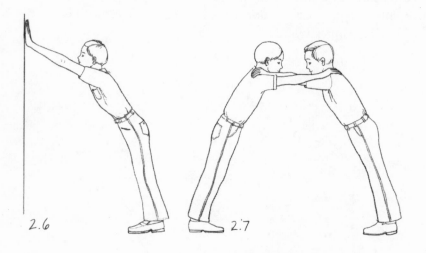

2.6   2.7

3
What Is a Beam?

SOME ELEMENTS OF A STRUCTURE DEVELOP BOTH TENSION AND compression at the same time. The most important of such elements is a *beam*. In a building, a beam is the horizontal structural element that connects the top of two columns. By putting together a group of vertical columns and connecting them with horizontal beams, we obtain the frame of a building: it looks like a jungle-gym (Fig. 3.1).

The beams, which are supported by the columns, support, in turn, the weight of the floors, and the floors support the weight of people and of all the furniture on them.

To find out why a beam develops *both* tension and compression, put a thin plastic or steel ruler on two books set a few inches apart. Then put a weight on the ruler, like a stone or a small book, or push down on it in the middle with your finger. You will notice that under the action of the weight or of your finger, the center of the ruler beam moves down, and the beam becomes curved. It *bends* (Fig. 3.2). Now get hold of a rectangular sponge, like those used in the kitchen, or a rectangular piece of foam rubber

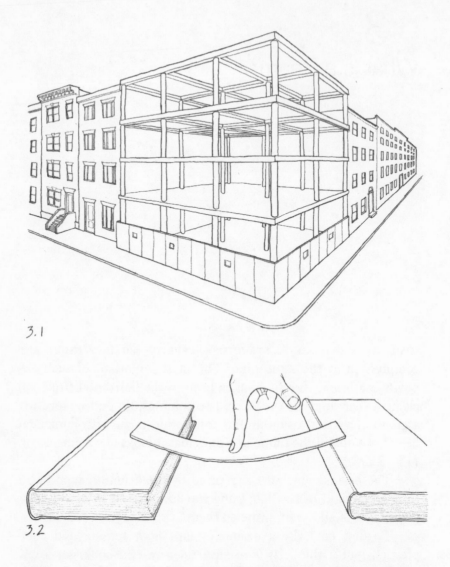

3.1

3.2

(the longer the better). With a magic marker, draw a set of vertical lines on one of its narrow sides and *bend* the ends up with your hands (Fig. 3.3). You will notice that the distance between the vertical lines shortens at the top and lengthens at the bottom of the sponge beam. Because tension lengthens and compression shortens, you will realize that in bending the beam up, the lower part of the

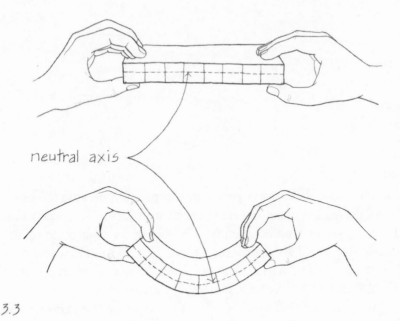

neutral axis

3.3

beam is put in tension and the upper part is put in compression. If, moreover, you draw with the marker a horizontal line halfway between the top and the bottom of the sponge side, you will notice that the distance between the vertical lines remains *unchanged* along this horizontal line and so does the length of the line. This means that along this horizontal line the beam develops neither tension nor compression. This is why the horizontal midway line is called the *neutral axis* of the beam. The ruler under your finger's pressure behaved like a bent sponge beam too, but the lengthening and shortening at its bottom and top edges were so tiny you could not see them.

If you hold the sponge with one hand and push down the free end of the sponge with the other hand, you will notice that the vertical lines *spread apart at the top edge and gather together at the bottom edge.* In such a beam, which we call a *cantilever* (Fig. 3.4) and which is supported at one end only, the upper part of the beam

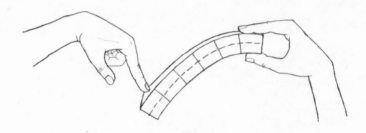

3.4

is in tension and the lower part is in compression because the beam curves down, but there is a neutral axis in it just as in a beam that curves up at one or both ends. The balconies of a building are usually supported by cantilever beams (Fig. 3.5). However, they do not bend as much as a piece of sponge because they are made of very stiff materials, like steel, concrete or wood.

In a framed building the beams are bent by the loads on the floors, and the columns are compressed by the beams. The entire frame works together because the loads on the building develop compression in the columns and bending (which is both compression and tension) in the beams.

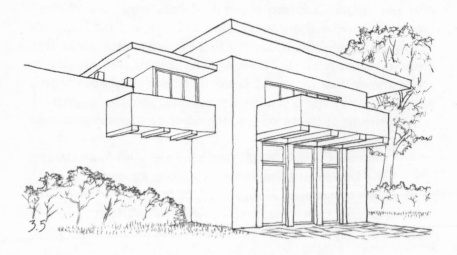

3.5

4

What Do We Build Structures With?

SINCE ALL PARTS OF A STRUCTURE ARE EITHER IN TENSION OR IN compression, or both, the materials used to build structures must, first of all, be strong in tension, in compression, or in both.

In nature there are many materials strong in compression: stones of all kinds, for example. To make sure that the stones will stay one on top of the other, they are "glued" with *mortar*, a mixture of lime, sand and water that looks like a paste when it is just mixed, but becomes hard as stone in about a week (Fig. 4.1). Among stones, marble is one of the strongest and that is why many columns and walls were built of marble in ancient times, and some still are today (Fig. 4.2).

The Romans, who were the greatest road and bridge builders of antiquity, built their arch bridges of stone. Since, as you know, the pieces of an arch work in compression, stone is the right material for arches because of its great compressive strength (Fig. 4.3). The Romans "glued" the arch stones with good mortar. Some of the bridges in Rome today are 2,000 years old and yet can carry the heavy loads of modern traffic.

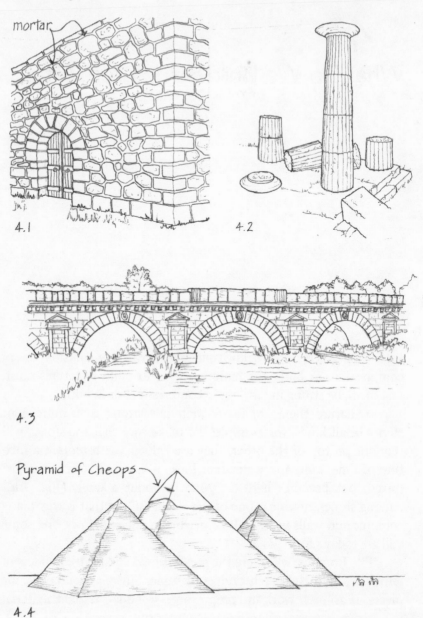

4.1

4.2

4.3

4.4

The Egyptians built their pyramids out of stone. The biggest of them all, the Pyramid of Cheops (Fig. 4.4) is 482 feet tall and is made of 2 million blocks of limestone that weigh 2 tons to 4 thousand pounds each. It looks like a mountain.

Since the Egyptians had no steel tools, how could they have cut these heavy blocks out of the mountain stone quarries? They did it by cutting slits in the limestone using tools made of diorite, a stone harder than limestone, and then pushing wood wedges into the slits. When the wood wedges were wetted with water, they swelled up and split the stone from the walls of the quarry (Fig. 4.5). The Egyptians were able to do this because stone is strong in

4.5

compression but *weak in tension,* so it could be wedged apart.

There are many man-made materials that behave like stone. Bricks, made out of burned clay, are so strong in compression that we can use them to build columns or walls 25 to 30 stories high. Many arch bridges of the Middle Ages were also made out of brick and are still able to carry today's traffic (Fig. 4.6).

Concrete is a man-made material, a mixture of water, sand,

4.6

small stones and a gray powder called cement, that hardens to full strength in four weeks. It is very strong in compression because it is very compact: The grains of sand fill the voids between the stones and the paste of cement and water fills the voids between the grains of sand (Fig. 4.7). The cement, which glues the sand and the stones together, is made by burning limestone and clay till they fuse and grinding the cooled mixture into powder in a big mill. Concrete made with good cement and stones, sand and water in the right proportions can be stronger in compression than most natural stones. But, like bricks and stone, concrete is weak in tension.

Though stone, brick and concrete are good materials to build columns or arches with, they are not well-suited to build beams, as some part of a beam is always in tension. Beams of concrete, when heavily loaded, show vertical cracks near the bottom because the tension there pulls the concrete apart (Fig. 4.8).

A common natural material strong both in compression and in tension is wood. The strongest man-made material—much stronger than wood and equally strong in tension and compression —is steel. This is why you see columns as well as beams of wood (these beams are often called *joists*) in one-family houses whose floors span not more than 20 feet and do not carry heavy loads (Fig. 4.9), but steel columns and beams in office buildings or in-

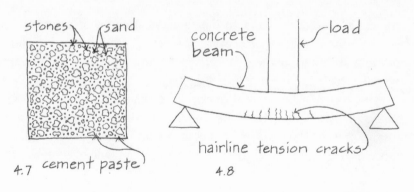

stones, sand

4.7 cement paste

concrete beam

load

hairline tension cracks

4.8

4.9

dustrial factories that must carry heavy loads over much longer spans. Aluminum is as strong as steel both in tension and in compression, although it is 3 times lighter. However, aluminum is much more expensive than steel.

There is a most ingenious way of combining two materials,

concrete and steel, in order to increase the strength of a concrete beam. You remember that because concrete is weak in tension the bottom part of a concrete beam cracks, due to the tension developed there when it bends (see Fig. 4.8).

If a concrete beam is in danger of cracking at the bottom it can be "stitched" together with steel bars that, being strong in tension, prevent the cracks from occurring or opening wider if they do occur (Fig. 4.10). Such beams are said to be made of *reinforced*

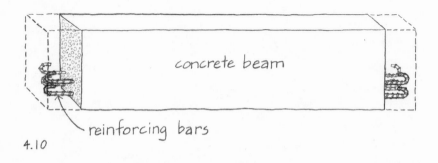

concrete beam

reinforcing bars

4.10

concrete and are now used in all concrete buildings. (The first example of reinforced concrete is found in a beam over the door of a Roman tomb dated 100 B.C. It is reinforced with bronze rods.)

To get a feel for what the steel reinforcement does in a concrete beam, you can perform a simple experiment. Out of a Styrofoam slab a quarter of an inch thick, cut a beam about 1 inch wide and 2 feet long. If you hold one end of the beam in your hand you get a cantilever that will bend downward because of its own weight (Fig. 4.11a). It will bend down even more if you push on its free end. Since the cantilever curves down, its upper part is in tension and its lower part in compression. Take a piece of Scotch tape and tape it along the top of the Styrofoam cantilever (Fig. 4.11b), and then repeat the experiment. You will find that the deflection or bending down of the cantilever tip is much smaller. The Scotch tape is stiff in tension, much stiffer than the Styrofoam, and prevents the upper part of the foam cantilever from lengthening so much in tension. The tape thus reinforces the

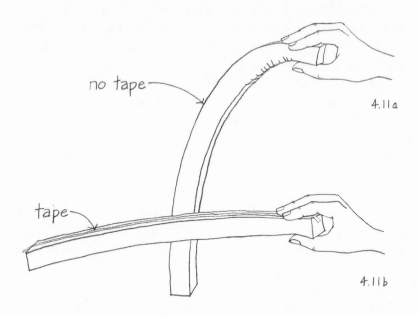

no tape

4.11a

tape

4.11b

Styrofoam. If you peel off the tape, the cantilever will droop again.

The steel bars in a concrete beam are much stiffer in tension than the concrete. Those in a cantilever beam act like the Scotch tape in the foam beam: they prevent the upper part of the concrete beam that is in tension from lengthening too much and cracking (Fig. 4.12).

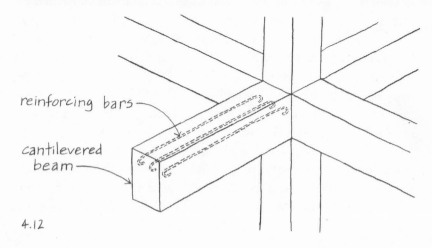

reinforcing bars

cantilevered beam

4.12

Reinforced concrete is a very good and inexpensive material because it uses a large amount of cheap concrete and a small amount of expensive steel. In addition, it is a *fire-retarded material.* Steel is very strong at normal temperatures, but if a fire develops in a steel-framed building, the columns and beams, even if covered with fire-insulating materials, may get hot, and if their temperature rises above 700° Fahrenheit, they lose their strength and melt. Concrete is in itself a good insulating material. It protects the steel from melting for a long time and so retards its failure. A reinforced concrete building is usually safer against fire than a steel building. Buildings with columns, beams and floors of reinforced concrete are built all over the world. The material is inexpensive and particularly well suited for apartment buildings. The tallest concrete building, the Water Tower Plaza building in Chicago, is 859 feet tall.

If structural materials are not strong enough in tension or compression or both, the beams and columns of a building will break under heavy floor loads and the building will collapse, possibly killing the people in it. Also, an arch bridge will collapse if its material is not strong enough in compression to support the weight of the traffic going over it. Once in a while such disasters occur. One of the largest steel roofs in the United States, over an ice hockey rink in Hartford, Connecticut, collapsed because it could not support an exceptionally heavy load of snow. Luckily, the hockey rink was not in use at the time. Its roof was supported on four large columns and measured 360 feet by 300 feet. It came down in a few seconds. The 2,800-feet-long suspension bridge over the Tacoma Narrows, in Tacoma, Washington, was destroyed by a steady wind that made it sway wildly. Its roadway collapsed after bending and twisting for 70 minutes (Fig. 4.13). Fortunately, these failures are most unusual and well-designed structures built with good materials do not collapse.

Strength is not all that is required of a good structural material. All materials, both tensile and compressive, must have another important characteristic called *elasticity.* Support the ends of a steel ruler on two chairs and push down on it. As you push, measure,

4.13

by means of another ruler set vertically near the middle point of the first, by how much its middle point goes down, or *deflects* (Fig. 4.14a). Let us say that under a slight push the ruler deflects by one quarter of an inch. If you stop pushing, the deflection disappears (Fig. 4.14b). Increase the push and you will measure a larger deflection, say, half an inch. And if you stop pushing, the deflection disappears again. Whenever the deflection disappears when you stop pushing, we say that the ruler behaves *elastically*. (As you can see, a rubber band is correctly called an elastic, because if you stop pulling on it, it returns to its original length.)

However, if you increase the downwards push on the steel ruler so much that a kink appears in it at the mid-point, you will find that the deflection (and the kink) do *not* disappear when you stop pushing (Fig. 4.15a, b, c).

Elasticity, therefore, is a required characteristic of all structural materials. Even when they deflect under a load, and they all do since there are no perfectly *rigid* materials, the deflection should disappear when they are unloaded. If a kink were to appear in a steel beam supporting a floor, and if every time after that when we put on a heavier load the kink and the deflection were to increase, the floor would soon become unsafe and unusable, because half of it would be sloped down and half of it up.

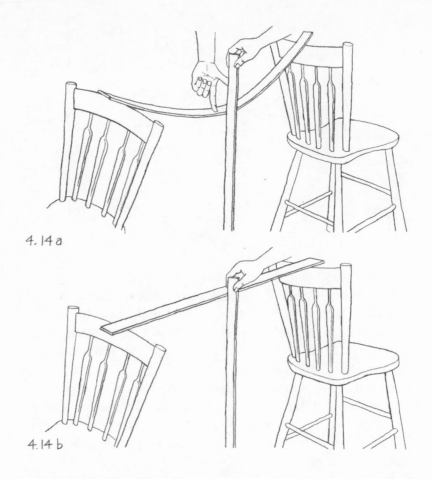

4. 14 a

4. 14 b

Of course, no material is elastic forever: if you keep on increasing the load on it, eventually it breaks. And that's the end of it as a structural material. But, before it breaks, the material may develop a *permanent deflection*, like the kinked ruler, and then we say, in structures, that it is not elastic anymore, it behaves *plastically*. (The word "plastic" has two different meanings, one in chemistry and one in structures. In chemistry, "plastic" is a noun and means a man-made material like nylon or celluloid. In structures, "plastic" is an adjective and means not elastic any more.)

Plastic behavior under heavy loads is also necessary in struc-

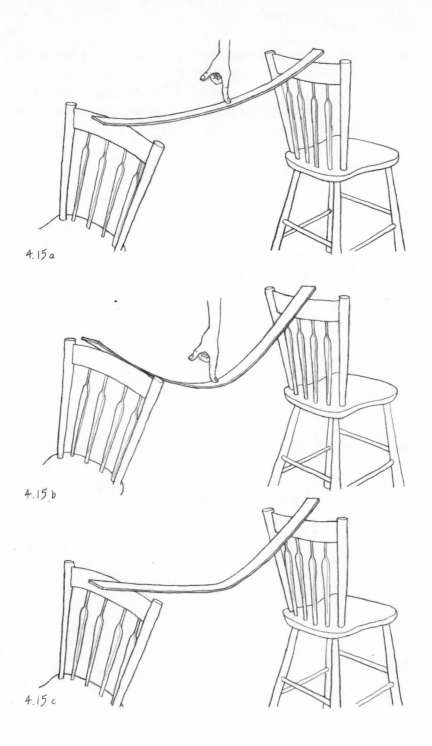

4.15 a

4.15 b

4.15 c

tural materials. Among other things, it acts as a safety device. Its appearance gives advance warning of collapse. When a structural material begins to behave plastically and a permanent deflection appears, it is a warning sign that the material cannot support a much greater load without collapsing entirely.

5

The Floor of Your Room

IF THE EARTH DID NOT PULL, IF THE WIND DID NOT BLOW, IF THE earth's crust did not shake and the air temperature did not change, we would not need structures in buildings. Buildings would stand up by themselves. But the pull of the earth, the force of the wind, the shaking of the earth's crust, which causes earthquakes, and the expansions and contractions due to temperature changes exert loads and forces on all buildings, and these must be resisted by means of the structure.

When you are in your room, look around and notice how many things rest on the floor. Can you guess how much they weigh? (Fig. 5.1) Let's suppose you yourself weigh at least 80 pounds, two chairs 15 pounds, your bed 100 pounds, the chest of drawers 100 pounds, the book shelves with the books 65 pounds, and the desk 80 pounds. So far the weights add up to 440 pounds. All these loads are called the *live load* on the floor, because, like your own weight, they can be moved around as if they were alive. To make sure the floor will not collapse, we must make it strong enough to support the live load, and here we run into a problem. Perhaps you are alone

dead load – walls
ceiling
floor
windows

live load – furniture
people
books & clothes

5.1

in your room today, but tomorrow could be your birthday, you could give a party and have ten people in the room. The weight of people then would not be your own weight only but ten or more times that much. Your books may grow in number as you collect more of them. You may decide to move your desk to a new location. In view of all these uncertainties about the live load, the building department of your city decides what is the largest live load that may be put on your floor and publishes a book called the *Building Code* which tells the engineer for what live load he *must* design the floor. Of course, the code plays it very safe. To show you how safe it plays, let's do a little calculation. Let's assume that during a party you have 10 friends in your room and that they weigh about 100 pounds each, or all together 1,000 pounds. Adding their weight to the 440 pounds we computed when you were alone, we get 1,440 pounds of live load.

If your floor is 12 feet wide and 15 feet long, the floor surface is 180 square feet (12 feet by 15 feet). This means that your floor consists of 180 squares measuring 1 foot on each side (Fig. 5.2). If the live load of 1,440 pounds were evenly spread over the floor and each square carried the same load, each square foot of floor would be loaded with 8 pounds (1,440 divided by 180). This would be the "even" live load per square foot carried by the floor of your room during the party.

A load evenly carried by the floor is called a *uniformly distributed load* and is measured in pounds per square foot. If you are an engineer you abbreviate this as psf. The uniformly distributed load on your floor would then be 8 psf.

It would be hard for you to guess what uniform live load most Building Codes want the engineer to plan for in his floor design: they require a *design live load* of 40 psf, which is 5 times as much as the load we have just figured out! When you deal with a floor, it is better to be safe than to have it collapse because people are together in one corner and the live load is not uniform. Who knows what loads may be put on your floor by another tenant? So, your floor is designed to support 40 times 180 or 7,200 pounds of live load.

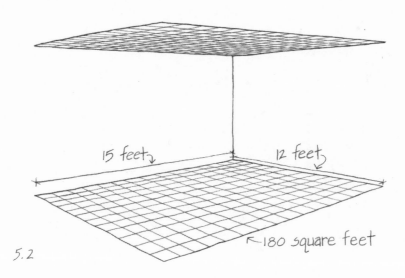

15 feet   12 feet

180 square feet

5.2

When it comes to the live load your roof must be designed to carry, its weight will depend on where your house is located. In New York or Philadelphia, as much as 30 psf of snow may fall on a roof, but in northern Canada, there may be 80 psf of snow (Fig. 5.3). The various building codes in each area tell the engineer what he must assume the snow load to be.

You may feel that 7,200 pounds of live load is a lot, but if in designing a floor you only considered the live load, you would forget the heaviest of all the loads on it: the weight of the floor itself. This is called the *dead load*, because it cannot move; it is always there, and it is very heavy. If you live in an apartment building with reinforced concrete floors, the floor load per square foot of floor is computed by taking into account the thickness of the floor and the weight of concrete for each cubic foot. It may be 100 psf, which is two and a half times as heavy as the code live load. We include in the dead load the floor load, the load of the floor tiles

5.3

(about 5 psf) and that of the thin walls or *partitions* between the rooms, since we don't know where they may be moved by a new tenant, but we know they will always be there. They are assumed to weigh about 20 psf. (The outside walls do not rest on the floor; they are supported by the outside beams of the frame.) So the *total load* per square foot of a floor could be, for example, 100 psf (floor load) + 20 psf (partitions) + 5 psf (floor tiles) + 40 psf (live load) = 165 psf. (You can abbreviate dead load as D.L., live load as L.L. and total load as T.L.) In this case, the *total design* or code load on the entire floor of your room would be 165 psf times 180 square feet or 29,700 pounds. If you want to calculate the total load on the floor of your room, measure the room (round off the number to the nearest foot), find the number of square feet (multiply length by width) and then multiply that by 165, if you live in a large apartment building. Otherwise, you might try to check the building code in your city or area, and use whatever figures it gives as the live load and the dead load. It is inconvenient to write and handle such big numbers as 29,700 pounds. To avoid the inconvenience, we usually measure big loads in *tons*. A ton weighs 2,000 pounds, so the total design load in tons on your floor is 29,700 divided by 2,000 or 14.85 tons.

In designing buildings, the evaluation of the loads on a floor is a careful and painstaking job. No one wants to fall through the floor because the engineer made a mistake in assessing the floor load. An Italian proverb says: "It is better to be cautious than to get hurt," and this could be taken as the motto of a good design engineer.

6

A Steel Frame . . . Made Out of Paper

THE BEST WAY TO UNDERSTAND HOW THE FRAME OF A BUILDING works is to build one. A good model of a steel frame can be built with paper, provided we first build the separate elements of the frame: the columns, the beams and the floors.

A column should not take too much floor room, but must be strong enough to carry the compressive loads without buckling under them. A column buckles, that is, bends under compression along its axis, if it is too thin. Take a plastic ruler, stand it up and push downward on it: there comes a point when the ruler will bend out (Fig. 6.1).

To avoid the danger of buckling, steel columns are built in the shape of a capital I (Fig. 6.2). To better understand why an I-column is strong and does not easily buckle, take two strips of paper 2 inches wide and 11 inches long, fold them along two lines ½ inch from their long edges (and hence 1 inch apart), and glue them back to back as shown in Figure 6.3. If you stand this paper I-column vertically and push on it, it will take some compressive load, while the two separate unfolded strips of paper could not even

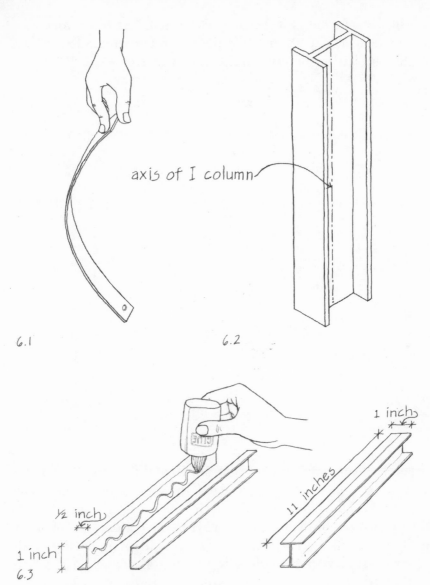

axis of I column

6.1

6.2

½ inch

1 inch

6.3

1 inch

11 inches

1 inch

stand up under their own weight. In general, a column becomes strong against buckling if its material is spread out away from its center line or axis.

To demonstrate a hollow square column, take a strip of paper

5 inches wide and 11 inches long. Draw on it, lengthwise, four lines, each one inch apart, and fold the paper along these lines. Then glue the last to the first 1-inch strip, as in Figure 6.4. While the

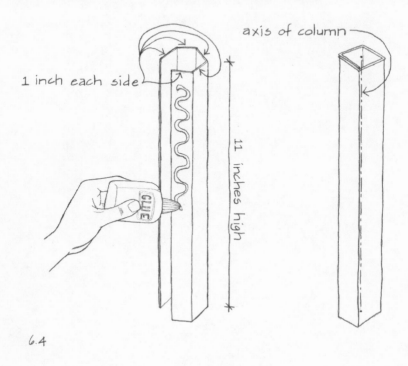

6.4

unfolded paper strip cannot carry any load, the square column can.

The more material is spread out, the stronger the column. The paper I-column can be made much stronger by glueing a 1-inch strip of paper to the top and another to the bottom sides of the I; these are called its *flanges* (Fig. 6.5a). However, if two 1-inch strips of paper are then glued to the vertical side of the I, which is called its *web* (Fig. 6.5b), the increase in strength against buckling is very little because the added material is near the column axis.

Since I-columns have fairly wide flanges and do not really look like capital I's they are called *wide flange sections*. They are labeled with a W and the product of two numbers, like W14x53. The first

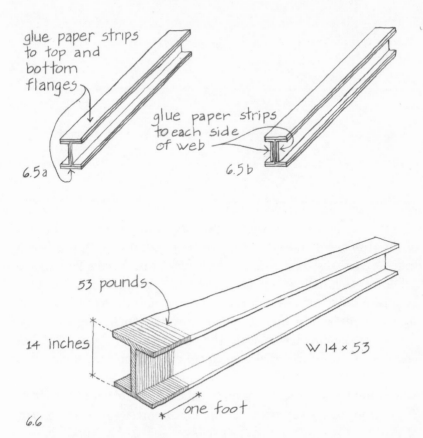

glue paper strips
to top and
bottom
flanges

glue paper strips
to each side
of web

6.5a

6.5b

53 pounds

14 inches

W 14 × 53

one foot

6.6

number measures their depth in inches and the second their weight in pounds for each foot of length. A W14x53 is 14 inches deep and weighs 5 lbs. per foot (Fig. 6.6). If the paper column of Figure 6 weighs 0.2 lbs. per foot it would be labeled W1x0.2.

If you cut a beam or a column at right angles to its axis, you see the shape of the beam's so-called *cross-section*. This can be rectangular, circular, triangular, I-shaped, and either full or hollow (see Fig. 6.7). The cross-section obtained by cutting the beam is a plane figure and its area is called the *cross-sectional area* of the beam or column. For example, a rectangular wood beam (a *joist*) 2 inches wide by 10 inches deep has a cross-sectional area of 20 square inches. Engineering handbooks listing the properties of wide-

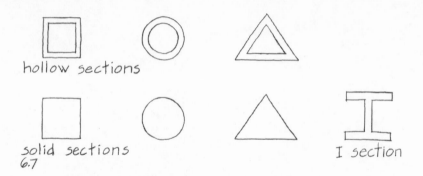

hollow sections

solid sections
6.7

I section

flange beams always include their cross-sectional area.

If you had a 5-inch wide paper strip, can you guess the shape of the strongest hollow column you could build with it, if a 1-inch width of strip is used to glue the paper? You would find that a column with a hollow *circular cross-section* would be the strongest, because *all* the material in it is as far away from the axis as possible. In a column with a hollow square cross-section having the same surface as the circular column, the corners are farthest away, but on an average the material is nearer the axis than in a circle (Fig. 6.8). If two hollow columns, one circular and one square, have the same outer surface and the same thickness, the circular one is about 20% stronger against buckling under compression. Another way of stating this result is to say that if we make the round column 20% thinner and hence lighter, it will be as strong as the square column. Unfortunately, circular columns cannot be used too often because it is difficult to connect them to beams.

To determine the most efficient section for a steel beam you must remember that a beam works in bending. The beam's lower part stretches in tension, its upper part shortens in compression and the neutral axis neither stretches nor shortens. This means that the steel *at* the neutral axis doesn't do any work and that the steel near it does very little work, while the steel farthest away from the neutral axis bears most of the burden of carrying the load. Because of this, it is efficient to take the material near the neutral axis (the middle axis of the beam) and put it as far away from it as possible. Figure 6.9 shows that if we start with a rectangular cross-section

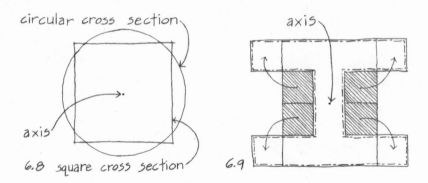

beam and take away the inefficient material near the neutral axis (the shaded part on the diagram) and put it symmetrically above and below, we obtain a wide-flange section. It is not surprising, therefore, that steel beams have wide-flange sections, just like columns, and are labeled with the same symbols. For example, a W27x102 beam is 27 inches deep and weighs 102 lbs. per foot of length. Of course, since bending efficiency depends on distance from the neutral axis, beam cross-sections are usually deeper than column cross-sections, while column cross-sections are chunkier than beam cross-sections, since they work in compression rather than in bending.

To experiment, make two wide-flange beams, as shown in Figure 6.3, one with a ½ inch deep web and one with a 1 inch deep web. Use glued strips of paper as you did in making columns. You will see that the deeper beam is much stiffer than the shallow beam even though they have the same flange width (Fig. 6.10). You may also experiment using a steel or plastic ruler as a cantilever beam. With the width of the ruler in a horizontal position, push down on its free end. You will find how much stiffer it is if you push down on its free end when the width is vertical. (This is so, because in the ruler with the width vertical more material is farther away vertically from the neutral axis.)

Floors have to be flat and smooth so people can walk on them. In concrete buildings floors are usually made by pouring concrete on a horizontal platform of wood (called the *formwork*) and reinforcing it with steel bars set mostly at the bottom of the slab thus

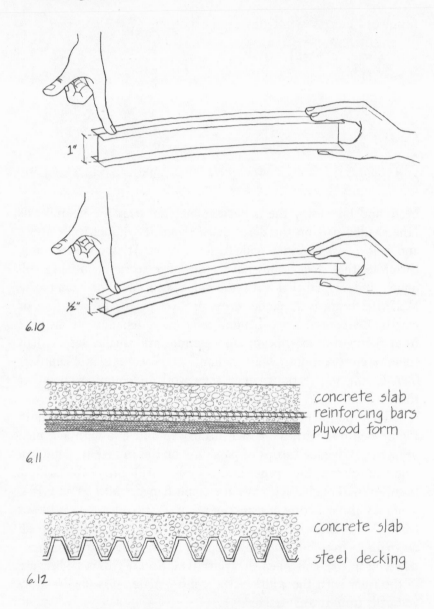

1"

½"

6.10

concrete slab
reinforcing bars
plywood form

6.11

concrete slab

steel decking

6.12

built (Fig. 6.11). In steel buildings, most often, instead of a platform of wood, a *steel deck*, which is a wavy platform of steel, is
used. It works both as formwork to support the concrete before it
hardens and as steel reinforcement for it (Fig. 6.12). The wavy

formwork creates small ribs at the bottom of the concrete slab, which stiffen it.

In your model paper frame the concrete floor slabs may be represented by cardboard slabs. If the cardboard is thick enough, it can easily support the loads of model furniture and people.

To put together a frame one must build a sufficient number of columns, beams and floor slabs and then connect them. In practice most steel beams and columns are connected by means of angles and bolts, as shown in Figure 6.13a. The bolts must be very tight and strong and are called *high strength bolts*. In certain frames the beams and columns are *welded* to each other by melting a welding material at the connections (Fig. 6.13b), but bolted connections are as strong as welded connections.

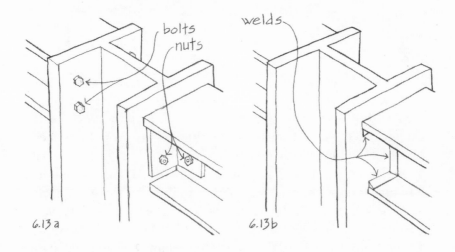

bolts
nuts

welds

6.13 a

6.13 b

Reinforced concrete frames look like steel frames, but have columns, beams and floor slabs made of concrete poured into wooden or steel forms. In *flat slab* construction the slabs rest directly on the columns without intermediate beams (Fig. 6.14).

In your paper model you may glue the columns to a cardboard base, using short strips of adhesive paper or Scotch tape or stamp hinges, and then glue the beams to the columns in the same way,

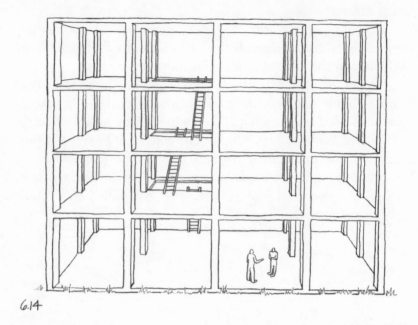

6.14

as shown in Figure 6.15. The cardboard floors are laid on the beams, after cutting out small squares at their corners to allow for the columns of the next floor to go up (Fig. 6.16). To put together a two-story building with floor dimensions of 11x5½ inches with only one room per floor you need 4 columns, 11 inches tall, and 8 beams, four of them 11 inches long and four of them 5½ inches long. All beams and columns can be 1 inch deep and 1 inch wide. You will need two floor slabs, 5½ inches by 11 inches. The second slab is really the roof slab. Figure 6.16 shows the finished frame without the roof.

To complete the building you need to enclose the frame with walls, in which there are windows and doors. In a model building you can draw windows and doors on paper walls and glue the walls to the frame. In your model the walls would be 5½ in. by 11 in. rectangles on the long sides, and 5½ in. by 5½ in. squares on the short sides of the building. Four of each are needed, two for each floor.

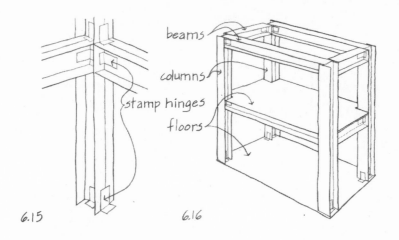

beams

columns

stamp hinges

floors

6.15   6.16

In actual buildings, the outside walls do not have to be very strong, since they must carry only their own weight and a small amount of wind pressure. They are made of brick or cement blocks, or often of thin aluminum or steel plates, which allow larger wall openings, since they are stronger than brick or block (Fig. 6.17). In some modern buildings the window panes are so large that the entire facade is made of glass attached to thin vertical columns of steel, aluminum or concrete called *mullions*. These facades are

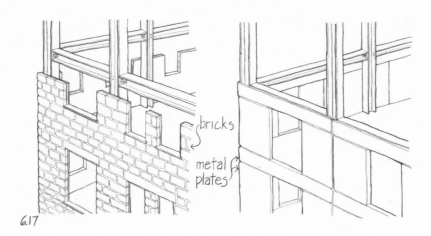

bricks

metal plates

6.17

6.18

incapable of carrying loads and are therefore called *curtain-walls* (Fig. 6.18).

As you walk the streets of a town, you can see many buildings under construction. In the downtown sections of our cities many steel-framed buildings go up, and by looking carefully you can see the details of the frame and the walls as described in this chapter. Figure 6.19 shows one such building, with its columns, beams, floors and their connections.

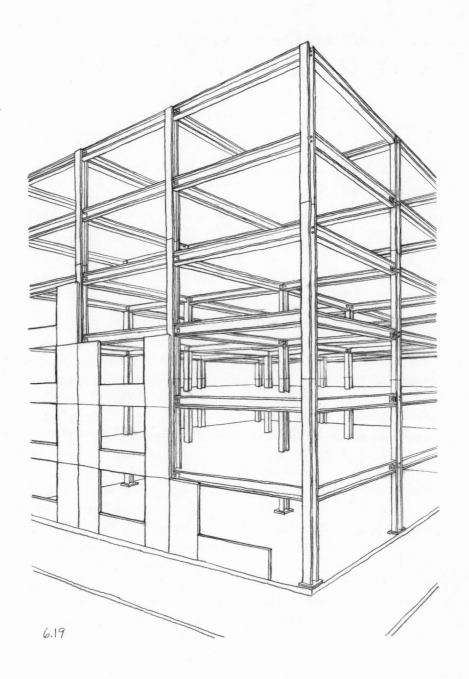

6.19

7

The Part of the Building You Don't See

THE CONSTRUCTION OF A LARGE BUILDING IS USUALLY STARTED BY making a big hole in the ground. This excavation has two purposes: to reach a layer of soil or rock strong enough to support the building, and to allow the construction of one or more basements and sub-basements in order to get the most use out of the expensive building lot. In Manhattan, a borough of New York City, a building lot can cost as much as $600 per square foot or $8,640,000 for a standard 120 ft. × 120 ft. lot. To find out how strong the soil is at various depths, engineers take samples of the soil by means of deep borings and test them in soil mechanics laboratories.

By law the contractor must put up a barrier around the building lot, but people are so curious about what goes on behind it that very often the contractor puts holes in the barrier at various heights for men, women and children to "kibitz." What the onlookers see is large excavators and shovels or cranes scooping up the earth and loading it onto trucks. At times, they hear explosions of dynamite that break up the rock at the bottom of the excavation. When the bottom of the excavation has been made flat, large square blocks of concrete are poured at the spots where the columns are going to go up. These so-called *footings* support and distribute to the ground the loads coming down to earth through all the columns built one on top of the other (Fig. 7.1).

When the soil is of clay or shale rather than rock or sand, it is weak. The footings may then become so large in order to distribute the building's weight over a wide area, that they touch each other and they become a single *foundation slab* of concrete (Fig. 7.2). There are soils, made out of a mixture of sand and water, that are so weak the foundation slab has to be made hollow

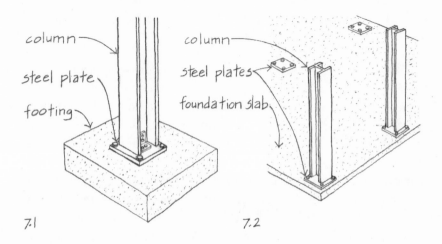

7.1   7.2

so that it literally floats in the almost liquid soil (Fig. 7.3). This is the case in the downtown section of Mexico, where the National Theater was originally built level with the central square, but slowly sank into the soil by as much as 6 feet. Then, shortly after the theater started sinking, a lot of high-rise buildings were built all around it, and their weight on the soil pushed the theater up above the level of the square, where it safely stands. The concrete frame of the theater moved integrally down and up without damage.

Often soil is uneven in strength and may give in more on one side of the building than on another. This is what happened to the

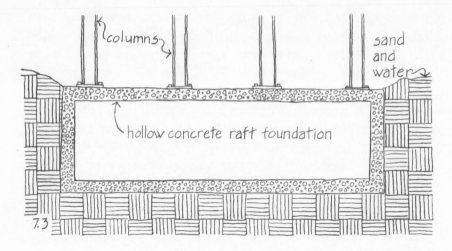

191-foot Leaning Tower of Pisa in Italy from the very beginning of its construction in the 14th century. The Pisans thought they could solve this problem by continuing the construction of the tower at a steeper upward angle than the leaning lower part and so balance it (Fig. 7.4). But this did not stop the tower from moving on its foundation. The top of the tower, which is 16 feet out of plumb (or line) goes over about 1 inch every 8 years. The Pisans are now trying to decide how to stop this motion before the tower falls over. They want to leave it in a stable *leaning* position, to make sure it will lean no further, but still lean. Who would go to Pisa to look at the tower, beautiful as it is, if it were straight?

If you look at an excavation in weak soil you may often see long round poles of wood, concrete or steel, called *piles*, being driven into the soil by a noisy *pile driver* that repeatedly drops a heavy weight on the top of the pile until the pile reaches solid soil or rock or cannot be pushed down any further. When the pile is tightly gripped by the solid soil, it is called a *friction pile* (Fig. 7.5a); when the pile is supported by rock it is called a *bearing pile* (Fig. 7.5b). The footings or the slab can then be built over the piles, which support them.

The loads on the footings can be very, very heavy when the building is tall. Calculating the load is a simple arithmetical job.

7.4

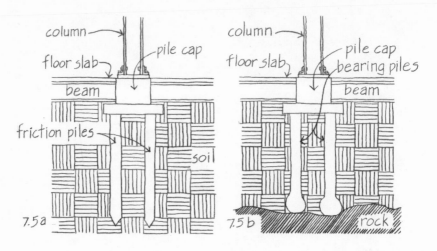

Imagine that the columns of a building are set 20 feet apart in both directions, so that each column carries the load on 20 ft. by 20 ft. or 400 square feet of each floor (Fig.7.6). If, as we found in Chapter 5, each square foot of the floor carries a total load of 165 lbs., 400 square feet of each floor will carry 400 sq. ft. by 165 psf or 66,000 lbs. of load. As 66,000 divided by 2,000 is 33 tons, each column carries 33 tons per floor. For a building with 40 stories, the total load accumulated at the bottom of each column would be 33 tons per story times 40 stories, or 1,380 tons. If the building were as tall as the Sears Tower in Chicago, which has 120 stories, the load on the footing at the bottom of each column would be 33 tons per story times 120 stories, or 3,960 tons. You need solid soil to carry such loads. At times such strong soil is only found many feet into the earth; heavy, hollow steel cylinders, called *caissons*, are driven very deep into the ground and filled with concrete to support these huge weights (Fig. 7.7). The towers of suspension bridges are very often supported on caissons driven below the level of the water.

Once the structure is built, nobody sees the foundations and it is easy to forget they exist; but they are there and they are perhaps the most important part of any building. Remember this next time you see a building or bridge, and remember also that if they are complex and costly it is to prevent structural failures, most of which are due to faulty foundations; a building is only as strong as its foundations.

Take a look through one of the peepholes next time you walk past a construction site. It can be fascinating, especially when you know what's really going on.

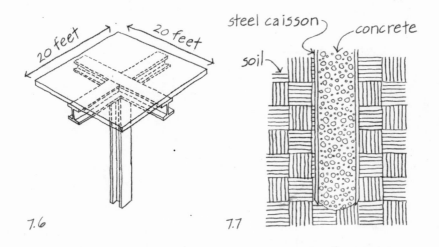

7.6

7.7

8

What Tornadoes, Earthquakes and Temperature Can Do

THE PURPOSE OF A BUILDING'S STRUCTURE IS TO GUARANTEE THAT the building will stand up under all the loads and forces acting on it: the weights, the pressure of the wind, the forces due to temperature changes, and, possibly, the shaking caused by earthquakes. The builders want to make sure that the building will not collapse, and they hope it will not even be damaged, since in the first case it may kill people and in the second it may be costly to repair. They also want to make sure that the building will not move around. If a house were to slide down the slope of the hill it is built on, or if a skyscraper were to be toppled by the wind, the buildings would have failed their purpose, even if their structures might sometimes end up undamaged.

When a building does not move we say that it is in *equilibrium*. (Equilibrium is a Latin word meaning "balance.") If you slide this book on your desk by pushing on it, the book is undamaged, but it moves (Fig. 8.1a). It is not in equilibrium. If you stand the book on your desk and topple it with your hand, the book may still be undamaged, but it falls. It is not in equilibrium (Fig. 8.1b).

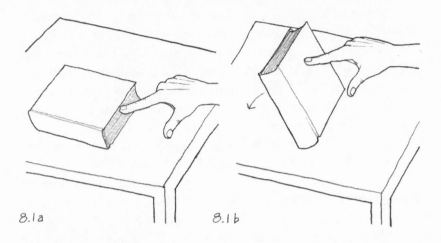

8.1a   8.1b

The laws of equilibrium were established by Isaac Newton over three hundred years ago. They simply require that for each force applied to the building an equal force should oppose it.

If you push toward the left on your book with your right hand, the book will move to the left. But if, at the same time, you push equally on it toward the right with your left hand, the two equal and opposite forces you exert on the book with your hands *cancel each other*, and the book does not move. It is in equilibrium (Fig. 8.2). Similarly, if you stand on the floor, your weight, *i.e.*, the force of gravity, tries to move you downwards, but the floor prevents this by pushing up or *reacting* on the soles of your feet and you are in equilibrium. If the floor were to give in, there would be no upward reaction to cancel the downward action of your weight, and you would fall.

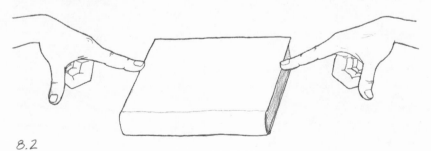

8.2

The same is true for a building. Its own weight and the weights of all the people and things in it try to move the building down, but the soil reacts upward on its foundation and keeps it in equilibrium (Fig. 8.3). If the soil is not strong enough to react and equilibrate the loads, the building sinks into the ground. A well-designed foundation guarantees that the building will not move up or down, that the building will be in *vertical* equilibrium.

If winds did not blow on buildings and if earthquakes did not shake them, all that we would have to worry about would be vertical equilibrium. To appreciate what a strong wind can do to a building, all we need is an empty cereal box, a piece of sandpaper, some sand or a few stones, and a fan or hair drier.

To represent a low building built on slippery soil (like wet clay), set the box on a smooth table with one of its long, narrow ends resting on it. Start the fan to blow a "wind" on one of the vertical broad sides of the box. If the wind is strong enough, the box will slide on the table, just as the building would slide on wet clay. The building would not be in equilibrium *horizontally*. To prevent such horizontal motion, it must be sunk deeply into the ground so that the soil can react horizontally against its foundation (Fig. 8.4). If a shallow foundation is used, it must be drained or the water pumped out of it, since dry clay is not slippery.

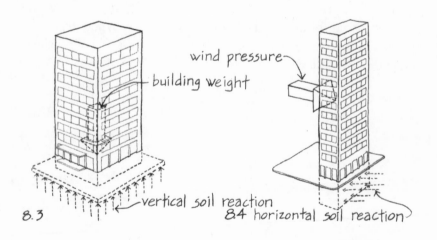

wind pressure

building weight

8.3   vertical soil reaction

8.4 horizontal soil reaction

To simulate the action of dry clay soil, put a piece of sand-paper under the cereal box and start the fan. The roughness of the sandpaper prevents the box from slipping because it develops friction between the box and the table, just as the roughness of the dry clay prevents the slipping of the building. The force due to friction reacts against the wind force and the two forces cancel each other out. The box and the building are in horizontal equilibrium.

Now set the empty box on the sandpaper with one of its short, narrow ends down, and start the fan. The box will not slide, but if the "wind" is strong enough the box will topple over by *turning* about the far edge of its base (Fig. 8.5). The box did not move

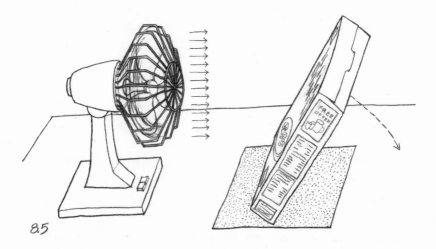

8.5

horizontally on its base, but it did turn and fall over. If you repeat this experiment after filling the box with enough sand or stones, you will find that, strong as the "wind" may be, the box will not fall or *rotate*. It is in equilibrium both horizontally and *rotationally*.

To understand rotational equilibrium you must remember how a seesaw works. If two children of about the same weight sit at the ends of a seesaw, the seesaw does not turn up or down at either end. It is in rotational equilibrium (Fig. 8.6a). But if a child plays on the seesaw with its father, in order to keep the plank from going down on the father's side because he is much heavier, the

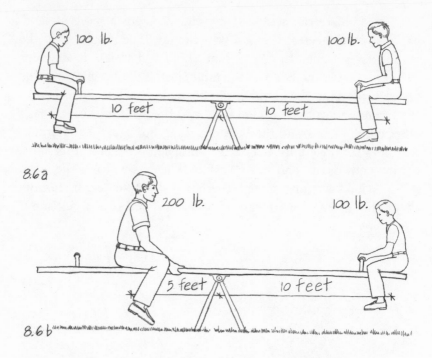

8.6a

8.6b

father must sit nearer the seesaw's center or pivot (Fig. 8.6b). For example, if the child weighs 100 pounds and his father 200 pounds, and if the ends of the seesaw are 10 feet from the pivot, the father must sit 5 feet from the pivot (Fig. 8.6b). Notice that in this case rotational equilibrium is obtained when the *product of the weight times the distance* from the pivot is the same for the child and the father. For the child the product is 100 lbs. times 10 ft. or 1,000 foot-pounds, for the father it is 200 lbs. times 5 ft. or 1,000 foot-pounds. We abbreviate feet times pounds as foot-pounds or ft.-lbs. If one product is larger than the other, the seesaw will be out of balance and will begin to turn.

The rotational equilibrium of a building follows the same rule. As the wind blows, the building tends to rotate around its lee-ward bottom edge (the bottom edge away from the wind) due to the product of the force of the wind times the vertical distance of the wind force from the edge (Fig. 8.7). But the dead load and the

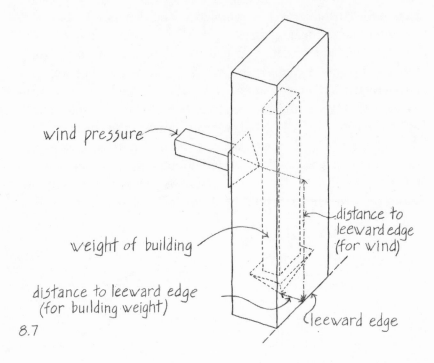

wind pressure

weight of building

distance to
leeward edge
(for wind)

distance to leeward edge
(for building weight)

8.7

leeward edge

live loads of the building, that is, its total weight, tends to rotate the building in the opposite direction, through its horizontal distance from the edge (Fig. 8.7). If the weight times its distance from the edge is larger than the wind force times its distance, the weight wins and the building does not topple over. In the cereal box experiment, when the box is full of sand or stones, even though the distance of their weight from the edge is smaller than that of the fan force from the edge, they make the box so heavy that they win and the box does not fall. It is in rotational equilibrium. When the box is empty, its weight is so small that the wind force prevails and the box falls over. It is not in rotational equilibrium.

To imitate an earthquake, jerk the sandpaper under the box back and forth on the table. The box will topple over easily when it is empty. You will have to jerk the sandpaper harder to make the heavy box fall but it will topple too. This shows that a heavy earthquake acts very much like an exceptionally strong wind. In fact, both earthquakes and tornadoes can overturn buildings if they don't break them up first.

It is perhaps puzzling, at first, to think that we must worry about temperature changes in designing a structure. But we must not forget that everything expands when heated and contracts when cooled. Columns, for example, become longer (and slightly wider) when exposed to high temperatures and shorter (and slightly narrower) when exposed to low temperatures. This is why the columns *inside* an air-conditioned building maintain more or less the same length, but those *outside* become longer in summer and shorter in winter. Figure 8.8 shows how the beams connecting

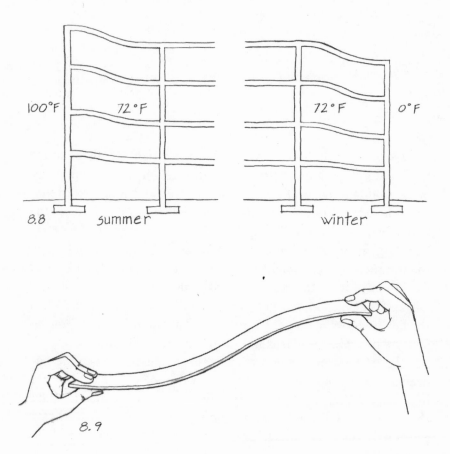

100°F   72°F   72°F   0°F

8.8   summer   winter

8.9

the inside to the outside columns must *bend* in opposite directions to follow these changes in length. Unless the beams are strong enough to take this bending, they may well break and the building may collapse. To "feel" this phenomenon, hold a plastic ruler in your hands and lift one end above the other (Fig. 8.9). If you lift one hand too much you may easily break the ruler.

9

How to Fight
Tornadoes and Earthquakes

THE HORIZONTAL FORCE ON A BUILDING DUE TO THE WIND DEPENDS on the wind velocity. The faster the wind, the greater the force. A wind blowing at 50 miles per hour (mph) produces a pressure of 7.5 pounds on each square foot of the building facade. A wind of 100 mph, twice as fast, produces a pressure 4 times larger: 30 psf (pounds per square foot). The total wind force from a 100 mph wind on the side of a giant skyscraper 120 ft. wide and 1400 ft. high is enormous, as shown by simple arithmetic. The side has an area of 120 ft. times 1400 ft., or 168,000 square feet, and at a pressure of 30 psf, the force is 168,000 sq. ft. times 30 psf or 5,040,000 lbs. This is 5,040,000 divided by 2,000 or 2,520 tons of wind force! As this horizontal force acts, approximately, halfway up the building, its vertical distance from the building's base edge is 1,764,000 feet times tons or feet-tons! Add to this the fact that the wind speed increases with height. The wind blows faster at the top of the skyscraper than at street level. It is no wonder that the wind becomes one of the most important considerations in skyscraper design.

The wind force consists of two separate forces: a pressure on the windward side and a suction on the leeward side. You can demonstrate this by attaching to two opposite wide sides of a cereal box a number of pieces of thread, either by glueing one end to the box or by threading them through two holes with a needle (Fig. 9.1). When the fan blows on one side, the threads on that side stick to it, but those on the other are sucked out from it (Fig. 9.2). This happens because the air must go around the

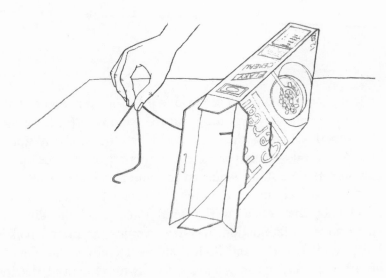

9.1

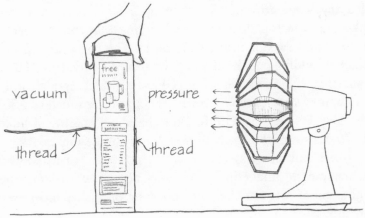

9.2

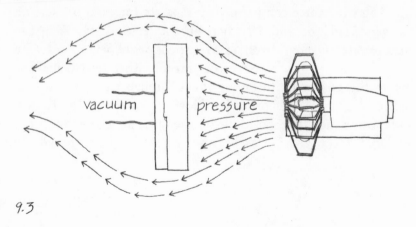

vacuum   pressure

9.3

building and creates a vacuum behind it, as shown in Figure 9.3.

If the wind is very strong and the windows of a building are not properly designed, the wind pressure on the windward side may push the window panes in, and the suction on the leeward side may suck them out, as happened to some of the glass panes in the John Hancock Insurance Building in Boston a few years ago.

Under the action of the wind force a tall building, well-anchored to its foundation, acts like a vertical cantilever stuck into the ground. It bends and its top moves laterally in the directions of either or both its sides (Fig. 9.4); its movement at the top is called the *wind drift*. If the building is too flexible, the people working in the top floors of the building may get "air sick" as the building sways in strong wind gusts. The wind drift in a well-designed building equals, at most, its height divided by 500. This means that the Sears Tower in Chicago, which is almost 1,500 ft. high, may sway back and forth at its top by as much as 1,500 ft. divided by 500, or 3 ft. On the other hand, an apartment building with 20 stories of 10 ft. each, may only sway by 4.8 inches.

If we look at a skyscraper we do not perceive its wind drift and its swaying under the wind gusts because of its tremendous height, but if we work on the top floor of a skyscraper we can sometimes feel the swings. Each swing takes a number of seconds,

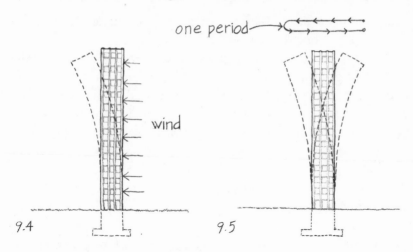

one period

9.4   wind   9.5

called the *period* of the building, which increases with the building's height (Fig. 9.5). The World Trade Center buildings in New York are about 1,400 ft. high and take about 7 seconds for a complete swing, from 3 ft. in one direction to 3 ft. in the opposite direction *and back*. You may think of a skyscraper as an upside down pendulum. Build a pendulum by attaching a weight or a stone at the end of a string and swing it. The longer the string, the longer the time for a complete swing, or its period (Fig. 9.6).

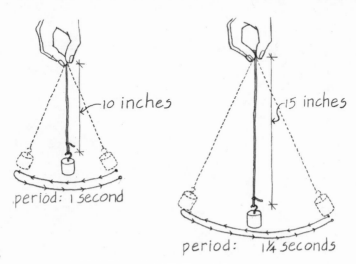

10 inches

period: 1 second

15 inches

period: 1¼ seconds

9.6

The same happens in buildings: in general, the higher the building, the longer a complete swing will take.

Back in 1620 the Italian physicist Galileo noticed, by looking at the swings of a chandelier in the Baptistry of the town of Pisa, that the period did not depend on how wide the swing of the chandelier was. A small swing takes as long as a wide one since during a small swing the pendulum moves slowly and during a large swing it moves fast, because in the large swing the pendulum falls from a greater height (Fig. 9.7). (You may check this with your stone and string pendulum.) The same holds true for the swings of a skyscraper, but when the swings are small they are almost unnoticeable.

To limit the swings of a building, it must be made stiff in bending. If you take the end of a plastic ruler in one hand and keep it vertical with the free end up, you can simulate the swings of a skyscraper by pulling on its free end and letting go. The ruler will swing, or *oscillate*. If you use a more flexible steel ruler, its oscillations will be slower. It is so important to stiffen a skyscraper against wind oscillations that often one-third of its steel weight goes to stiffen it. In a *high-rise building*, as skyscrapers are called today, this amounts to thousands of tons of steel and millions of dollars. This is why engineers have invented an ingenious device,

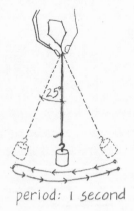
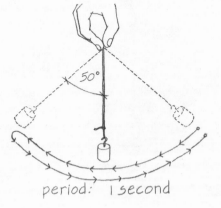

period: 1 second   period: 1 second

9.7

called a *tuned mass damper*, that reduces the oscillations of a building without increasing its weight substantially.

The tuned mass damper consists of a large block of concrete built under a shelter on the building's roof and attached to two opposite walls of the building by springs (Fig. 9.8). The damper

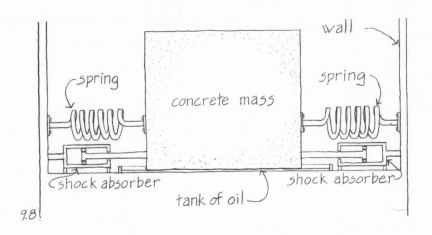

can slide with respect to the building in a shallow tank over a thin layer of oil. The weight of the concrete block and the stiffness of the springs are so chosen that when the building oscillates with its own period, the concrete block oscillates *with the same period as the building*. (This is why the damper is called "tuned": its oscillations are "in step" with those of the building.)

Now imagine that a gust of wind sways the top of the building to the left. As the concrete block is not *rigidly* attached to the building, it does not move and lets the building slide to the left under it (Fig. 9.9a). In so doing, it lengthens the left spring and shortens the right so that these springs pull and push the building back toward its center position (Fig. 9.9b). Moreover, this return motion is braked by shock-absorbers, so that the building stops at the center position under the concrete mass without swinging past it, as it would if it acted as a free pendulum. Its oscillations are "damped" by the tuned mass damper. A concrete block of only

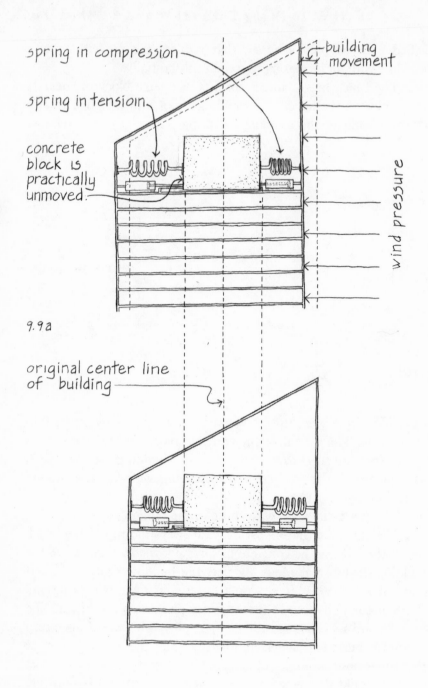

spring in compression

spring in tension

concrete block is practically unmoved.

building movement

wind pressure

9.9 a

original center line of building

9.9 b

a few hundred tons can make a building weighing thousands of tons stiffer without using much additional weight of steel. (Structural engineers have taken the idea of tuned mass dampers from mechanical engineers. Your car has four or more mass dampers to reduce its vibrations.)

The Citicorp Center building in New York has a 400-ton tuned mass damper at its top and it is the first high rise building so wind-damped in New York. The Hancock Insurance Building in Boston was equipped with two dampers after many of its window panes popped out or were damaged by wind oscillations.

The effect of an earthquake on a building is simliar to that of a strong horizontal wind, but it is much more dangerous because even a "sudden" wind gust is smooth in comparison with the jerks of an earthquake. A jerk, a sudden change in the direction of motion or a sudden start or stop of motion, is equivalent to the sudden application of a force. You can prove this by yanking the piece of sandpaper set under the cereal box and noticing that the box topples in the direction opposite to the yank. It is as if a force had been applied to the box in the opposite direction. The heavier the box, the heavier this apparent suddenly applied force, which is called an *inertia force* (Fig. 9.10).

A suddenly applied force has a much greater effect than a slowly applied force. This is why by applying the weight of a

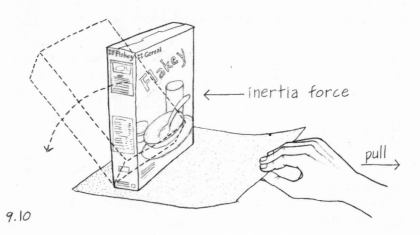

9.10

hammer suddenly to the head of a nail, *i.e.*, by hitting the nail on the head, the nail can penetrate a piece of wood. If you put the weight of the hammer gently on the nail's head, the nail doesn't even dent the wood (Fig. 9.11). The inertia forces due to earth-

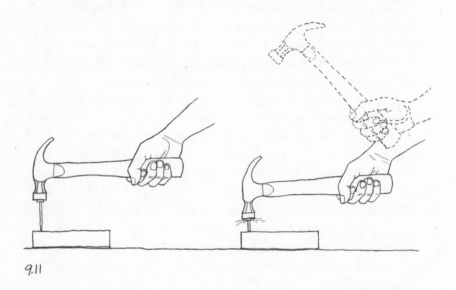

9.11

quakes are sudden or *dynamic forces*, because of the jerky motion of the earth's crust. Their effect can be catastrophic. To avoid collapse or great damage, buildings erected in earthquake areas must have much stronger structures to resist horizontal earthquake forces.

You may have heard that engineers and geologists are just beginning to forecast earthquakes. They can do this because during an earthquake one part of the earth's crust slides *suddenly* with respect to another adjoining part along a line called a *fault* (Fig. 9.12); but this only hapens if the earth's crust has been put under tremendous stress from within. If, by exploding a few sticks of dynamite in a hole deep in the earth's crust, we spread oscillations through the earth's crust, ripples or waves travel through it as they do when we drop a stone in a pond. It has been found that the speed of these waves changes when the stress in the crust changes. Thus, when we measure a change in the speed of the

9.12

waves, we know that the crust stress is changing and the crust may break, producing an earthquake. You can actually see the change in speed of waves due to changes in stress if you attach one end of a fairly long and heavy rope, say 15 feet long, to a doorknob or a tree and, while pulling on the other end, you wiggle it. Waves will travel from your hand toward the fixed end of the rope and the harder you pull, the faster they travel (Fig. 9.13).

It will be a great day for humanity when we can predict earthquakes well ahead of time, as some animals seem to be able to do naturally. In the last earthquake in the region of Peking, China, over one million people died.

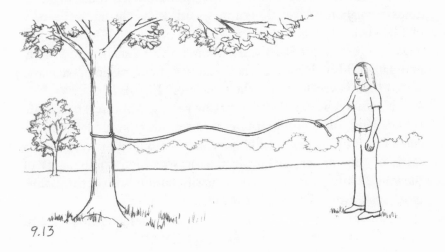

9.13

10
Ropes and Cables

WIRES AND STRINGS ARE SO FLEXIBLE THAT ONE WOULD NOT THINK they could be of much use in structures. But man's ingenuity has found ways and means of using materials strong in tension, by shaping them as thin, flexible ropes and cables, to build some of the largest structures in the world.

Natural vegetable fibers, like hemp, have been used for thousands of years to make strong ropes; with these the ancient sailors of Phoenicia, who first dared to enter the Atlantic Ocean, pulled on their sails against the strongest winds. With such ropes, Medieval knights lifted bridges that spanned their castle moats and locked themselves in against their enemies (Fig. 10.1).

Nowadays we build steel ropes by twisting thin steel wires into *strands* (Fig. 10.2) and wrapping steel strands around plastic nylon *cores* (Fig. 10.3). Such cables can only be pulled apart by thousands of tons of tension and are basic structural components of the longest bridges in the world: the suspension bridges that sometimes span over 5,000 feet between their tall towers.

To appreciate how a cable in tension carries loads, take a 3-ft.

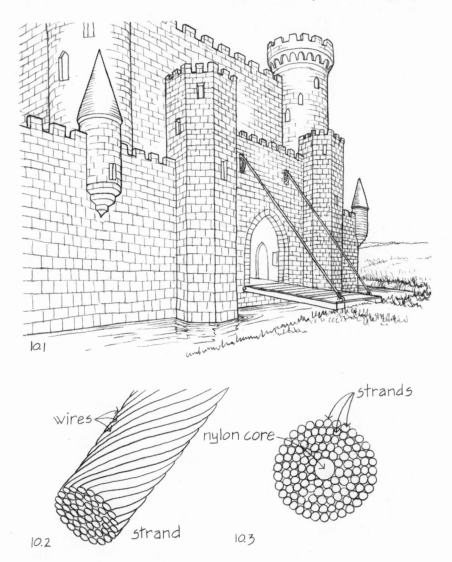

10.1

wires

strands

nylon core

strand

10.2   10.3

length of string and hang from it first one, then two, and then three weights. (If you do not have available scale weights, use a spool of thread or a small plastic bag full of stones or sand. These can be hung from the string as shown in Figure 10.4 so as not to slide along the string.)

If you hang one weight from the middle point of the string

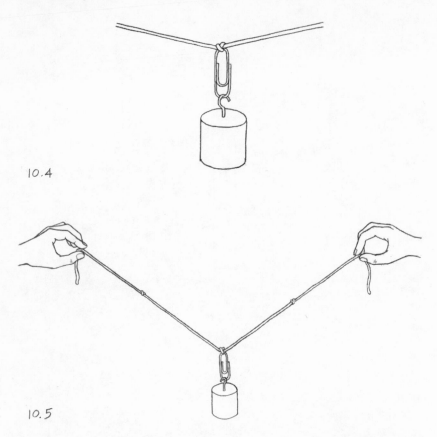

10.4

10.5

and lift the ends of the string, the two halves of the string become tensed and straight (Fig. 10.5). Notice that to lift the weight you must pull *up* on the string ends, so that the pulls up on the ends equal the pull down of the weight, but you must also pull *outward* on the string ends to keep them apart. The harder you pull outward on the string ends, the farther apart the ends will move, and the higher the weight will be lifted (Fig. 10.6). This outward horizontal pull on the string ends is called the *thrust* on the string. The string requires this *horizontal* force to carry the *vertical* weight. We call *sag* the vertical distance between the middle point of the string and the level of the string ends, and *span* the horizontal distance between the string ends (Fig. 10.6).

This demonstrates that the smaller the sag the stronger the

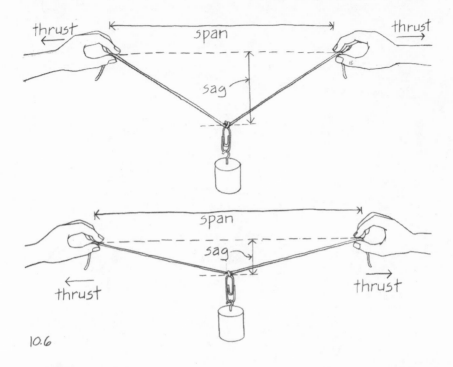

10.6

thrust in the string. Since a string is so thin that it cannot resist compression, and so flexible that it takes nothing to bend it, it can only develop tension. But it easily adapts its shape and its tension to carry the load whatever its sag. Of course, the larger and larger thrust needed to obtain smaller and smaller sags may eventually break the string.

To see how adaptable a string is, attach to it two or three loads. When you lift them, you will have to exert upward pulls and thrusts (outward pulls), just as you did in the case of one load, but you will notice that the string now takes a shape with three or four straight sides (Fig. 10.7). The shapes taken by a string always have straight sides between loads, since a string becomes straight when pulled by tension. These shapes are called *string polygons* (from the Greek "poly" meaning "many" and "gonia" meaning "angle"). These are shapes where each side makes an angle with the next (Fig. 10.7).

If one increases the number of loads attached to the string,

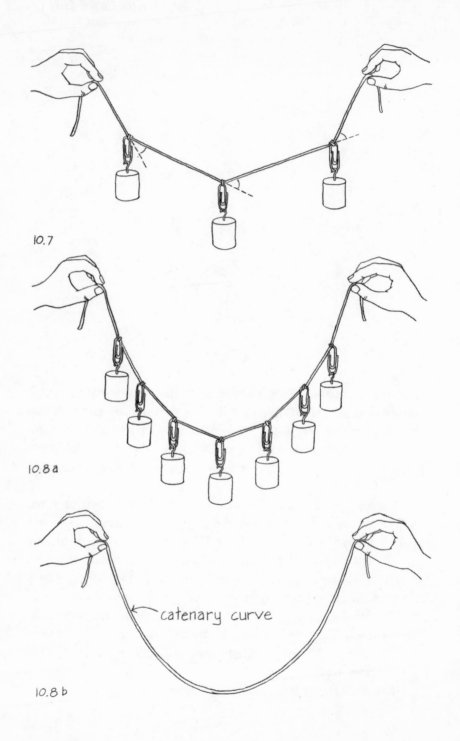

10.7

10.8 a

10.8 b

catenary curve

the straight sides between the loads increase in number and become shorter and shorter (Fig. 10.8a). Eventually the shape of the string becomes a *curve* (Fig. 10.8b). A curve is the shape assumed by the string when it hangs under its own weight (or dead load) only. Such a curve is called a *catenary* (from the Latin word for heavy chain or "catena"). If you imagine the string to consist of many small lengths of string attached to each other, you can see that the curved shape of the string is due to the many loads of *each* small length of string and that the weight of the string is equivalent to an infinitely large number of tiny loads hanging from it.

The adaptability of the string, which permits it to change shape when the loads change, is an advantage, as it makes possible the use of flexible ropes and cables to carry a variety of loads. On the other hand, the fact that ropes and cables change shape or, as we say, become *unstable* under varying loads is a disadvantage. In practice structures must maintain a fixed shape. How could one use a steel cable in a suspension bridge, if its shape were to change every time a truck goes over the bridge?

In reality cables must be *stabilized* or stiffened so as to make their change in shape under varying loads as small as possible. In a suspension bridge, cables are stabilized by hanging the roadway from the cables by means of *hangers* or suspenders and by stiffening the roadway by lateral trusses (Fig. 10.9), which act like stiff beams

hangers

stiffening truss

10.9

and maintain their horizontal shape even when loads move on the roadway. To demonstrate this, you can hang a stiff wooden ruler from a string by bits of strings of different lengths (Fig. 10.10); you can then place a small load anywhere along the ruler without noticeably changing the shape of the string.

A cable is called a *tensile structure*, because it can only work in tension, but one cannot build a "purely tensile" structure, that is, made out of cables only, since cables have to be hung from supports. A suspension bridge is an example of a working structure in which elements in tension (the cables), compression (the lateral towers), and bending (the stiffening trusses) are combined. Since a cable must have a sag in order to carry loads, the ends of the cables of a suspension bridge must be attached to two points high above the roadway. These are the tops of the *towers* of the bridge; the towers often stand in the bed of the river and are supported on *caissons* (see Ch. 7). If you remember that a horizontal thrust

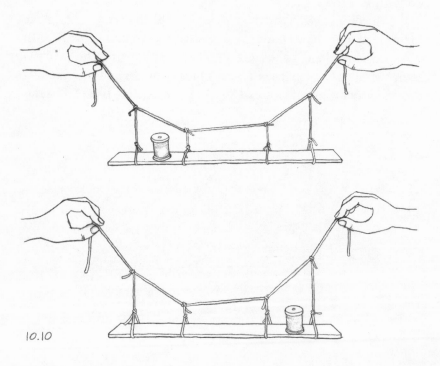

10.10

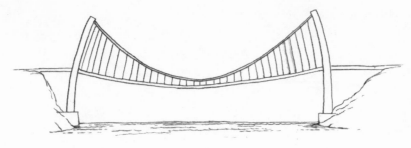

10.11 a

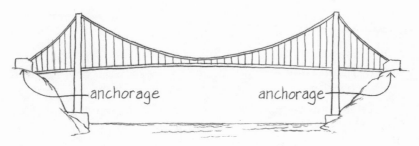

anchorage   anchorage

10.11 b

is applied at the ends of the cables, you will know that the thrust will *bend* the towers (Fig. 10.11a), unless you extend the cables on the other side of the towers and anchor them into the ground (Fig. 10.11b). To feel the difference between a cable that ends at the tower top and one that goes over it and continues to the ground, grab your head with your right hand and pull (Fig. 10.12a). If you try to keep your head straight, your neck will feel compressed, but also pulled to the right. Now intertwine the fingers of your hands, put them over your head and pull with both arms (Fig. 10.12b). Your head and neck will feel compressed, but your neck will not have to resist horizontally, since the thrust of your right arm is balanced by that of your left arm.

Thus, the towers of a suspension bridge work in compression rather than in bending. This is a big advantage, as a column in compression is much more efficient than one in bending. (As you

10.12 a   10.12 b

saw in Chapter 3, in bending, much of the material does not work at all.)

To anchor the ends of the cables, they are spread into enormous blocks of concrete poured into the ground and called *anchorages* (Fig. 10.11b).

To complete the bridge, the roadway with its *stiffening trusses* is hung from the cables by means of *suspenders* or hangers. We have seen that the stiffening trusses work like stiff beams in bending and we shall learn why they are called trusses in the next chapter.

It can be shown that since a fairly large sag reduces the cable thrust and therefore its tension, it also allows the cables to be smaller and thus less costly. The trouble is that to obtain a large sag, one would need very high towers, and the increased cost of the towers would more than balance the reduced cost of the cables. This is why the elegant shallow curve of suspension bridge cables has a small sag that is only about one twelfth of its span.

The longest bridge in the world was for many years the Verrazano Narrows Bridge over the entrance to the New York harbor. It has a span of 4,260 ft. between its towers and takes its name from that of the Italian explorer who first entered the New York bay in 1524. As of 1979, the longest suspension bridge in the world is the Humber Bridge in England, with a main span of 4,626 ft. In 1988, the Akashi-Kaikyo Bridge in Japan will become the longest, with a main span of 5,840 ft., or over a mile.

Since the cables of a long-span bridge have diameters of many feet and weigh thousands of pounds per foot, it would be practically impossible to lift the cables to the top of the towers. Instead, the cables are manufactured right on the towers by spinning their component wires back and forth from one tower to the other by means of a "spinning wheel" and by finally wrapping them together with a wire that spirals around them.

The crews capable of doing this job, at great speed and at heights of hundreds of feet above the level of the roadway, give a magnificent example of skill and daring. Because they are so highly skilled, they are greatly in demand and go all over the world, spinning cables for suspension bridges.

11
Sticks and Stones

WE HAVE SEEN IN THE LAST CHAPTER HOW A STRING CAN SUPPORT a load at its mid-span point by taking a shape with two straight sides (Fig. 11.1a). This is the simplest tensile structure that spans a distance. Can we obtain the same result with a compressive structure? The answer is that we can, by stiffening the two sides so that they will not buckle, and by flipping the string over so that its sag is above its span and becomes a *rise* (Fig. 11.1b).

If you take an old-fashioned nutcracker, with two arms hinged at the middle, and hang a weight from the hinge (Fig. 11.2), you will have such a compressive structure, which acts as a simple arch. You can "feel" how the nutcracker's arms are compressed by intertwining the fingers of your hands and resting your elbows on a table. If somebody pushes down on your hands, your arms "feel compression" (Fig. 11.3a).

Just as the tension in the string's sides, when a weight hangs down from it, becomes its opposite (compression) in the nutcracker sides, the thrust that pulls outward on the string's ends to prevent a reduction of the span, becomes in the nutcracker a thrust

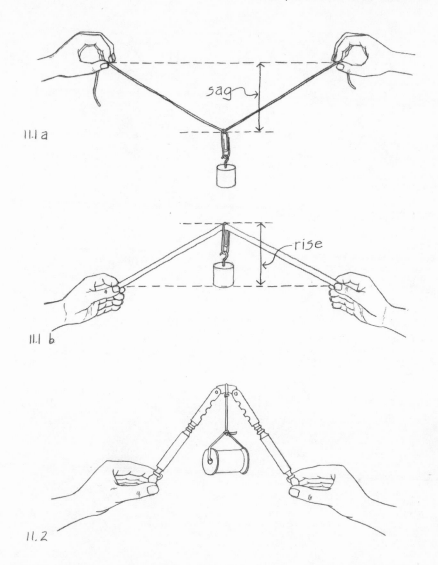

sag

rise

11.1 a

11.1 b

11.2

inward, which tries to prevent the span from opening up. To support a load, the nutcracker sides must be prevented from opening up by forces pushing *in* at its arms ends (Fig. 11.2).

Compressive structures with several sides can be similarly obtained by first hanging weights from a string and letting it take its tensile shape. If the shape is "frozen," by substituting com-

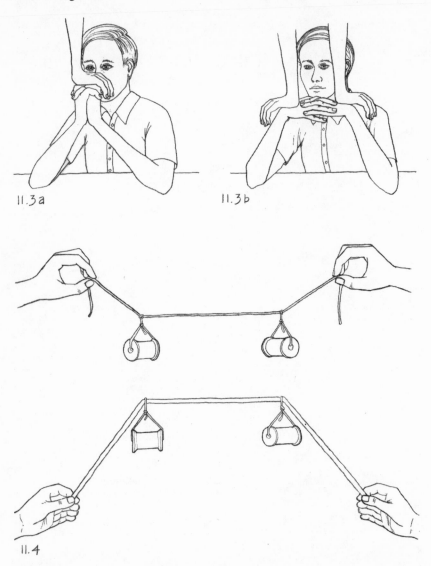

11.3a

11.3b

11.4

pressive bars for the string sides, and then flipped over, so that the sag is turned into a rise, and if the thrusts are reversed, a purely compressive structure is obtained. Figure 11.4 shows the compressive structure corresponding to the string shape under two symmetrical equal loads. You also can form a compressive structure like this by locking your hands together. If two downward forces are applied to your hands by someone pressing down on them, balancing inward thrusts must be supplied to the elbows, usually by the upper arms resting on the table (Fig. 11.3b).

Since wood is a good compressive material it is often used to build small bridges over brooks. The horizontal wooden beams of the roadway's surface are supported by four inclined wooden *struts* that meet at midspan (Fig. 11.5a) or *butt* into the beams at four separate points (Fig. 11.5b). Such bridges will stand up provided the struts can be supported by the brook's banks. If the banks are solid rock, the compressed struts will be safely supported by them,

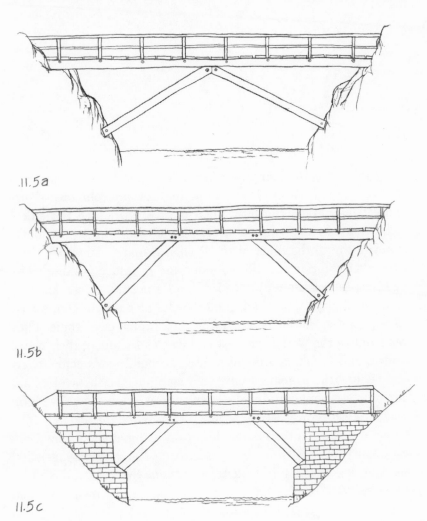

11.5a

11.5b

11.5c

but if the banks consist of a weak soil, the struts must be supported by *buttresses* of bricks or of concrete (Fig. 11.5c).

The natural tensile shape taken by a string or cable under its own weight is called a *catenary*. By flipping this shape up and "freezing" it, one obtains a curved *arch* (Fig. 11.6), in this case a *catenary* arch.

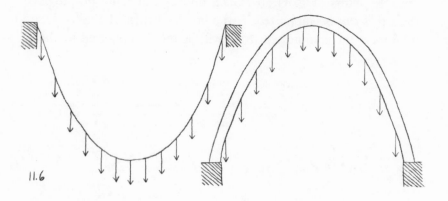

11.6

Arches are the compressive structures most commonly used to span large distances. They can be built of any compressive material: stone, brick, concrete, wood or steel. Although the oldest arch known to man was built around 400 B.C. (in Asia Minor), it was not until the times of the Roman Empire, 300 to 500 years later, that arches came into common use in bridge building. The Romans, whose empire extended from England, as we know it today, to today's Iraq, built 50,000 miles of roads to connect all corners of their far-flung domains to their capital city, Rome. They were among the world's greatest builders, and many of their roads, bridges and buildings are still in use. To build roads across rivers and ravines, the Romans always used arches in the shape of a half-circle. It was simple to build a semi-circular wooden formwork on which to wedge in place the stones, or *voussoirs*, for the arch. The stones were put on the wooden formwork symmetrically (one from each end), starting from both ends (called arch *springings*) and working toward the top. When the *keystone* that locked the others in place was set, the formwork could be taken down. You can

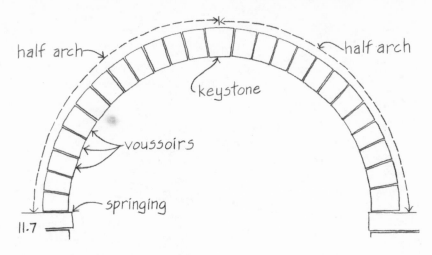

half arch

half arch

keystone

voussoirs

springing

11.7

think of an arch as consisting of two halves that lean one against the other at the keystone (Fig. 11.7). As Leonardo da Vinci, the universal genius of the 15th century, put it: "An arch consists of two weaknesses which, resting on each other, become a strength."

A bridge can be built by means of two parallel arches, above and beside which are erected walls up to the roadway, which become *parapets* above it (Fig. 11.8). The arches are connected by transverse beams over which the roadway runs. The Romans usually supported the roadway on wide *barrel vaults* (Fig. 11.9), which can be thought of as very wide arches or as a series of arches built one next to the other. Their bridges were built of such good stone, and with such good mortar to "glue" them together, that many of them stand up today and carry heavy loads after 2,000 years. Their spans reached 100 feet.

The Romans also built hundreds of miles of brick and stone aqueducts to carry water to their cities. These consisted of rectangular columns, called *piers*, carrying tiers of arches, over which ran the pipes for the water (Fig. 11.10). The tiers of arches were needed to allow long spans between the piers and to avoid having to build piers too tall and too heavy. Many of these structures can still be seen today around Rome, in southern France, and elsewhere in Europe and Asia Minor.

arches

parapet

11.8

11.9

The gothic cathedrals of the thirteenth century, with their pointed arches and *flying buttresses* (exterior half-arches), are perhaps the most glorious example of stone construction in the history of architecture.

The *gothic arches*, whose thrust is partly supported by the

11.10

flying buttresses (Fig. 11.11), allow the weight of the cathedral's roof to flow into the tall columns and piers, freeing the walls from their load-carrying role. Thus it was possible to open the walls with large stained-glass windows, which give the interior of the cathedral a luminous and airy feeling.

The cathedral's tall towers reach heights seldom before achieved, while their weight helps the stability of the structure. Built of carefully cut stone blocks, first by the master-masons of France, and later of England and Spain, the gothic cathedrals are a triumph of structural and architectural unity.

Modern arch bridges are built mostly of reinforced concrete and of steel. The concrete for the arches is poured into wooden forms, which are taken away once the concrete sets. Usually a concrete bridge consists of two arches supporting columns of varying lengths, which in turn support the roadway. The two arches are connected by straight struts of reinforced concrete crisscrossing each other, which make the arches work together against the lateral

11.11

11.12

push of the wind (Fig. 11.12). The longest concrete arch bridge in the world today is the Gladesville Bridge in Sidney, Australia, which spans almost 1,000 feet (Fig. 11.13).

Steel arch bridges are built of wide-flange shapes and work very much like concrete bridges. They have several advantages:

11.13

they are relatively light, and they require lighter foundations and lighter supporting structures, called *scaffolds*, during construction. They may be built without scaffolds by cantilevering each half and then connecting them at mid-span, and often they can be built more rapidly. The longest steel arch bridge in the world today is the New River Gorge Bridge in West Virginia. It spans 1,700 feet and is made of a special non-rusting steel (Corten), which does not

11.14

need to be painted every few years like ordinary steel (Fig. 11.14).

We cannot end this chapter on arches without mentioning the fact that, since steel resists tension just as well as compression, railroad and other bridges are sometimes built with inverted steel arches (Fig. 11.15), which behave as a tensile structure, since they have the shape of a cable. They are preferable when the bridge spans a deep gorge, as such bridges interfere less with the landscape. Their compressed roadway prevents the span ends from moving inward so that the cable-arch need not be anchored to the gorge banks, and is only supported by them.

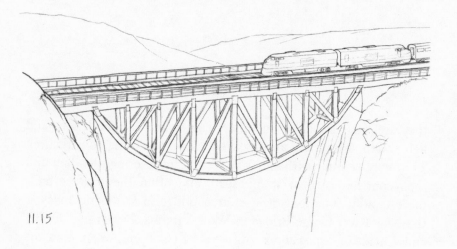

11.15

12
Strings and Sticks

IF USEFUL AND EFFICIENT STRUCTURES CAN BE BUILT USING *only* tension or *only* compression, as we have seen in the last two chapters, tension *and* compression members can also be combined to make some of the most useful structures ever invented by man. They are called *trusses* and have been used in many different ways for centuries.

One of the simplest and the most basic is a triangular truss. Remember that the purpose of the inward thrusts applied to the bottom ends of the nutcracker bars of Figure 11.2 was to keep them from spreading out. This result can also be achieved by tying these two ends with a string or *tie-rod*, thus making a triangular structure that does not require outside horizontal thrusts (Fig. 12.1). It is, so to say, self-contained and can be supported by vertical forces only, which balance the load on it and its dead load. The tie-rod is tensed by the tendency of the arms to open up. A simple *triangular truss* is made with two inclined compressive bars and one horizontal tension rod or bar. The roofs of many medieval churches, and of some modern one-family houses, are supported by such

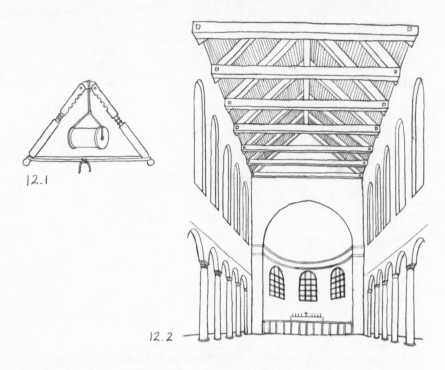

12.1

12.2

trusses with compressive bars of wood and tie-rods of wood or iron (Fig. 12.2). In some long span trusses, the sagging of the tie-rod under its own weight is reduced by supporting its mid-point from the top of the truss by means of a hanger (Fig. 12.3). In a truss

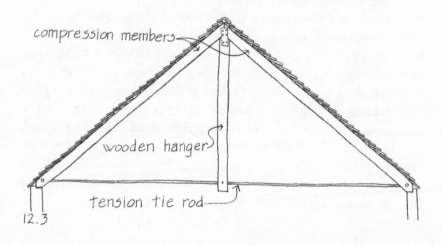

compression members

wooden hanger

tension tie rod

12.3

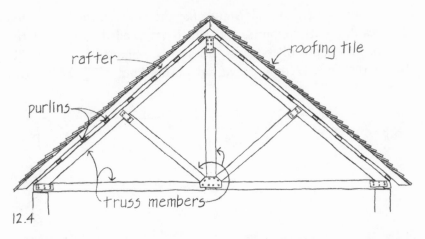

rafter

roofing tile

purlins

truss members

12.4

roof, a number of trusses parallel to each other support horizontal beams called *purlins*. On them are set the inclined *rafters*, on which planks of wood are nailed or flat or round tiles are set (Fig. 12.4).

The same type of trusses with wooden tie-rods are used to build small bridges, with the roadway resting on the tie-rod (Fig. 12.5).

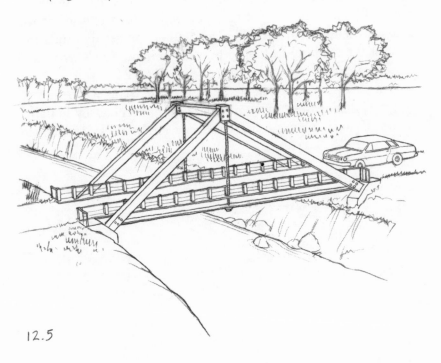

12.5

It is now easy to understand that the *outward* thrusts exerted on a cable by its supports, and which are needed to prevent the *inward* movement of its ends, can also be obtained by setting between the ends a compressive rod pushing out (Fig. 12.6): this

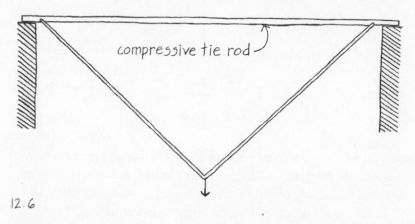

compressive tie rod

12.6

forms a triangular truss with two inclined tensile members and one horizontal compressive member. Small steel bridges are sometimes built this way, using either iron rods, cables or wide-flange sections as tensile elements. The horizontal member transmits the loads on the roadway to the bottom of the tensile rods by means of a vertical compressive bar called a *strut* (Fig. 12.7).

Large trusses can be made by connecting triangular trusses of the type just described. This may best be understood by building models of such trusses, using either ice cream sticks or wooden

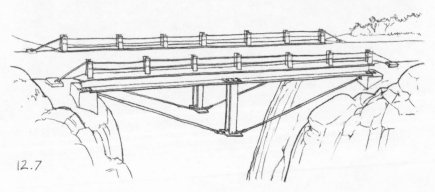

12.7

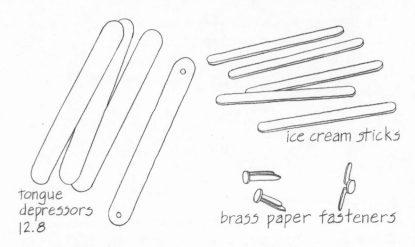

tongue
depressors
12.8

ice cream sticks

brass paper fasteners

tongue depressors (like those used by doctors), which can be
bought in boxes of a few hundred in any arts and crafts store. When
using tongue depressors, you must drill small holes at their ends;
this is best done by putting a number of them in a vise and drilling
through all of them at the same time. The only other parts needed
to connect the truss bars are small brass paper-fasteners, which
you can buy in stationery stores (Fig. 12.8). (Make sure when you
drill the hole that it is large enough for a paper fastener to go
through.) Ice cream sticks are too thin to be drilled and pinned
and should instead be glued together with Duco cement or with
glue.

To build a simple triangular truss, put a fastener through the
holes of two tongue depressors and open its arms (Fig. 12.9a). The
two bars are now connected, but *free to rotate* at the joint. Such a
connection is called a *hinge,* and the bars are said to be hinged.
Complete the triangular truss by means of a third bar hinged at
the ends of the other two (Fig. 12.9b). If you use the truss with a
joint or *vertex* above the horizontal bar and hang a load from its
top, the two inclined sides are compressed and the horizontal bar
is tensed. That this is so can be easily proved by substituting a string
for the horizontal bar, since we know that a string can only develop tension (Fig. 12.9c). If the triangle is inverted and the vertex

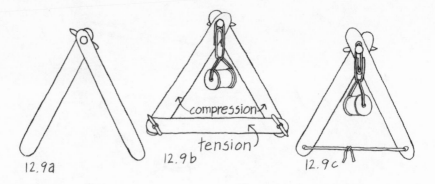

12.9a 12.9b 12.9c

is set below the horizontal bar, the bar which was in tension becomes compressed by a load hanging from the low joint and the compressed bars become tensed. If you substitute a string for the inclined bars (Fig. 12.10a, b), you can see that the string is in tension while the remaining horizontal bar is in compression.

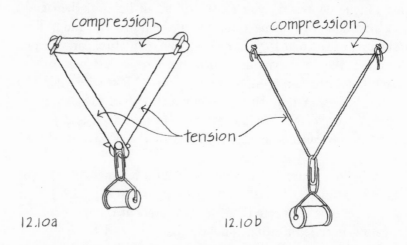

12.10a 12.10b

Now build two identical triangular trusses and connect, with a single fastener, one point of each truss (Fig. 12.11a). Since the two trusses are now hinged to one another, they cannot support loads. If the vertices are down, they tend to move apart (Fig. 12.11b). To prevent these motions and obtain a working truss, one more hinged bar is needed, connecting the two vertices. This addi-

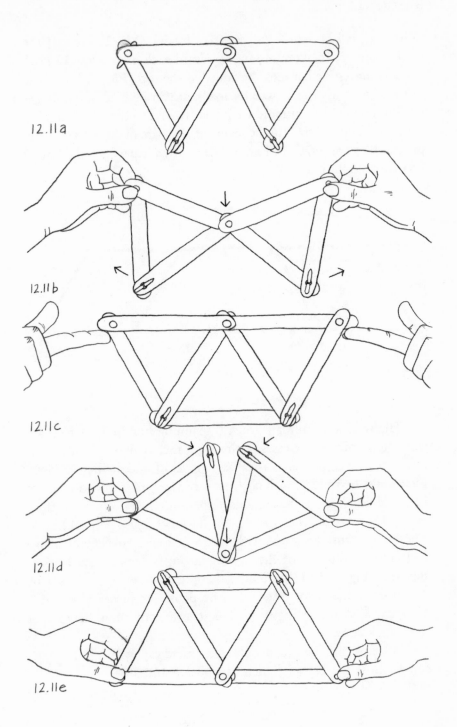

12.11a

12.11b

12.11c

12.11d

12.11e

tional bar will be tensile (try a string for it) (Fig. 12.11c). If the vertices are up, they tend to move toward each other (Fig. 12.11d) and a compressive bar must be added at the top (Fig. 12.11e). The new, longer truss can now carry loads. It can be made even longer by adding one or even more triangular trusses to the first two (Fig. 12.12). To emphasize the behavior of the bars of each truss, compressed bars are shown in Figure 12.12 with a heavy line and tensed bars with a light line.

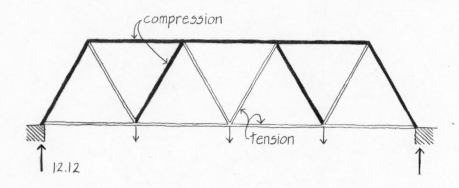

Highway and railroad bridges, spanning hundreds of feet, are very often built with trusses of this type, mostly made of steel bars. You can very easily make a realistic model of one of these bridges. First build two identical long trusses of the type shown in Figure 12.12. Hold them up and connect them at their top and bottom by transverse and crisscrossing or diagonal bars (Fig. 12.13a). These bars must be glued with Duco or a similar cement above and below the joints of the upper and lower bars of the truss as shown in Figure 12.13b. Finally, the glued connections should be stiffened by means of one-inch long depressor pieces glued at a 45° angle as shown in Figure 12.13b, so as to form small triangles at the connections.

A cardboard or glued depressors roadway will allow model cars to cross the bridge, which can be supported on two books or tables. A bridge model two or three feet long will not weigh more

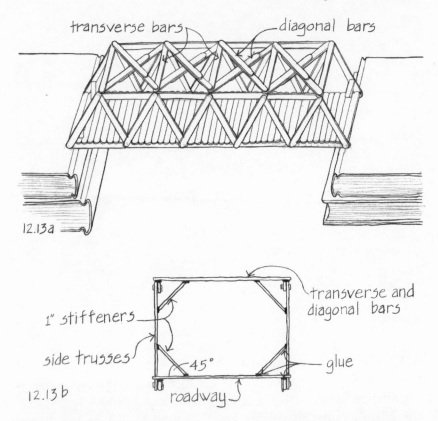

transverse bars   diagonal bars

12.13a

1" stiffeners

side trusses

12.13 b

transverse and diagonal bars

45°

glue

roadway

than a few ounces and yet can be loaded with a few pounds of books without collapsing. This proves how structurally efficient trusses are.

Figure 12.14 shows a few of the many other schemes of trusses used in modern bridge design.

Chapter 10 explained that stiffening trusses are used in suspension bridge design and that they act like stiff beams. It is now easy to understand why this is so. Notice first that in the scheme of the long truss on page 104 (Fig. 12.12), built of simple triangular trusses, when vertical loads are applied to it and the truss is supported at its ends, all the bars of the upper *chord*, that is, the upper horizontal bars, are compressed, while those of the lower *chord*, that is, the lower horizontal bars, are all tensed. Remember the behavior of a simply supported wide flange beam under vertical loads,

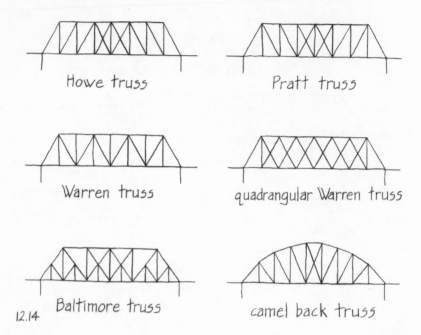

Howe truss

Pratt truss

Warren truss

quadrangular Warren truss

12.14 Baltimore truss

camel back truss

in Chapter 3; in that beam also the upper flange is compressed and the lower flange is tensed. A truss then behaves very much like a wide-flange beam, with the truss's upper chord or bars acting like the beam's upper flange, its lower chord like the beam's lower flange and its inclined bars, or *diagonals*, as the beam's web. The diagonals of the truss act like a web connecting the upper and lower flanges, but are lighter than a full web, because they form a web punched with triangular holes. The deep stiffening trusses in a suspension bridge are used to obtain great stiffness with a relatively small weight.

The stiffness of a truss is mostly due to the fact that it consists of triangles. You may check this by building a square out of hinged tongue depressors and noticing that it is easily deformed (Fig. 12.15a), but that it becomes quite rigid if a diagonal—cutting the square into two triangles—is pinned across it (Fig. 12.15b). (Make the diagonal out of two depressors, glued together lengthwise.)

The rigidity of triangulated trusses is often used to stiffen highrise buildings against the action of the wind. This is why in some

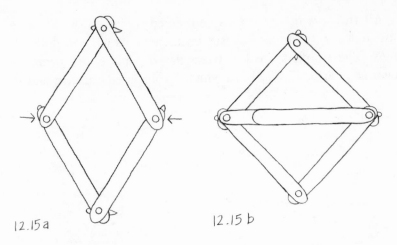

12.15 a   12.15 b

steel buildings the inner cage or *core* of the building, where the
elevators run, is made of four vertical trusses as high as the building, which act like cantilever beams sticking out of the foundations
(Fig. 12.16).

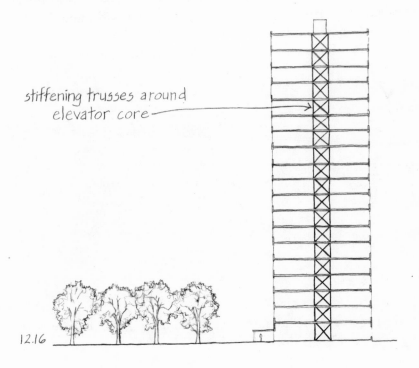

stiffening trusses around
   elevator core

12.16

All the bars of the trusses considered so far lie in the same plane, but a truss can also consist of hinged bars lying in different planes. The simplest are the triangular or square-base pyramids shown in Figures 12.17a, b, in which the inclined bars are said to

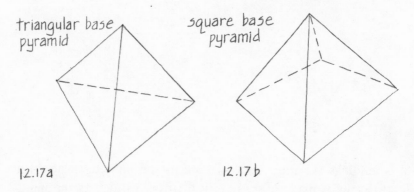

triangular base pyramid

square base pyramid

12.17a   12.17b

be *skewed* with respect to the horizontal bars of the base or *lower chord* of the pyramid. These pyramids can be combined to build so-called *space trusses*, which have bars in two horizontal planes, called the *upper* and *lower chord bars*, connected by skew diagonals (Fig. 12.18). Such space trusses of steel constitute the roofs of some

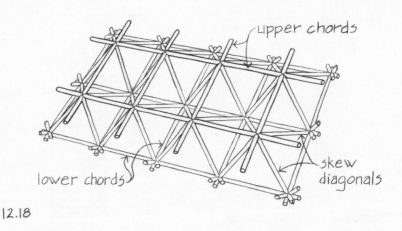

upper chords

lower chords

skew diagonals

12.18

of the largest sports stadiums and exhibition halls built to date.

Figure 12.19 shows the scheme of a Takenaka space truss,

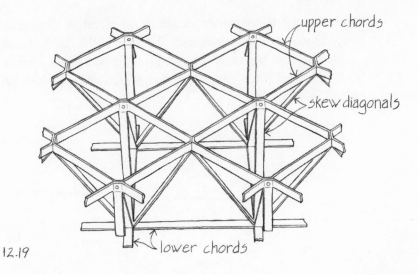

12.19

named after the Japanese company that patented it. It can be shown that under vertical loads hanging from it all the skew diagonals and all the lower chord bars of a Takenaka truss are in tension, while all the bars of the upper chord are in compression. A model of a Takenaka space truss can be built with ice-cream sticks for the compressed bars of the upper chord and strings for all the other bars (Fig. 12.20), following these step-by-step instructions.

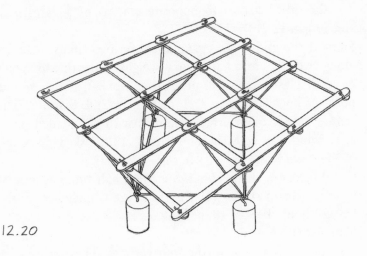

12.20

a. Form a square grid of ice cream sticks glued at their ends with Duco or similar cement. These are the bars of the upper chord of the truss. The grid should be 3 sticks long on each side and form 9 equal squares which you should label as in Figure 12.21.

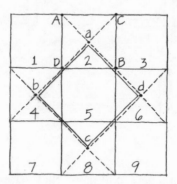

12.21

b. Cut 8 pieces of string two and a half times as long as an ice cream stick. (If your sticks are 6 inches long, the strings should be 15 inches long.)

c. Tie with a knot one end of a string to joint A and the other end of the string to joint B of square 2 (Fig. 12.21). Tie another string to joints C and D of square 2.

d. Tie the other strings to opposite corners of squares 4, 6 and 8 (Fig. 12.21).

e. Support the grid of ice cream sticks on two chairs or tables along two sides and hang equal weights (like thread spools or small plastic bags full of sand or stones) at the middle point of both strings in each of squares 2, 4, 6 and 8. The strings will form inverted pyramids with the loaded point a, b, c and d as vertices. The strings are the skew diagonals of the space truss.

f. Cut 4 pieces of string about one and a half times as long as your ice cream sticks. (If the sticks are 6 inches long, the strings should be 9 or 10 inches long.)

g. Connect the four loaded vertices a, b, c and d by tying the 4 strings with a knot to the four vertices. These strings are the bars of the lower chord.

This completes the Takenaka space truss.

If you support the truss on all four sides, you can hang slightly different loads from the 4 vertices and still have all string bars in tension and all ice cream bars in compression. Larger models of Takenaka trusses can be similarly built with 5, 7, 9 or more sticks to each side, possibly using tongue depressors, which are stronger than ice cream sticks.

In ending this chapter it must be mentioned that space trusses, built of stainless steel compressive pipes and thin steel cables, have entered the field of art. Kenneth Snelson, a New York sculptor, has invented (and patented) a structural system called Tensegrity with which he has built beautifully airy pieces of sculpture, some of them very large. They are shown in museums and outside areas all over the world. Figure 12.22 shows a large Tensegrity sculpture.

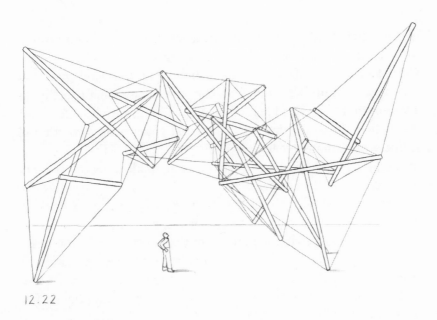

12.22

We all know that structures can be beautiful (think of a suspension bridge), but it took an artist to think of making beauty for beauty's sake out of trusses.

13
Shape and Strength

IF YOU HOLD A THIN SHEET OF PAPER BY ONE OF ITS SHORT SIDES, the sheet droops and is unable to carry even its own small weight (Fig. 13.1a). But if you bend it slightly upward and give it a *curvature*, it cantilevers out and may carry some small weight in addition to its own dead load (Fig. 13.1b). This simple experiment shows that the same amount of material changes its strength and stiffness depending on how it is shaped, and explains why some large curved structures can be built with small amounts of reinforced concrete, steel or plastics.

In the experiment with the sheet of paper, it is clear to those who remember how a beam works that, in curving the paper, we have moved some material away from the neutral axis of the cantilever, putting it above and below this axis, and hence, increasing its strength and stiffness. This is why large canopies of reinforced concrete, shaped this way and with a thickness of not more than a few inches, can be built over stadium stands, cantilevering 50 feet or more (Fig. 13.2).

Another way of emphasizing the strength that comes from

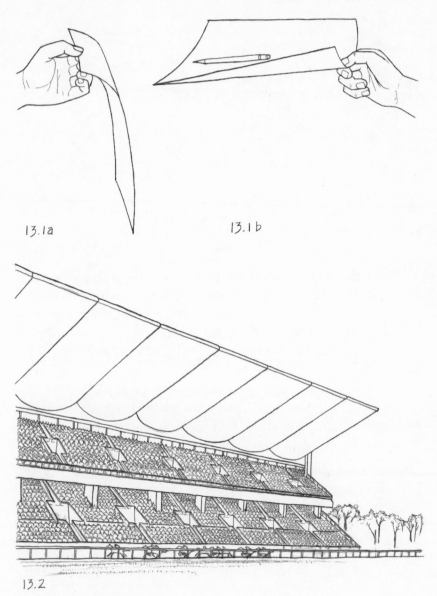

13.1a   13.1b

13.2

curvature is to try to span a distance of about 8 inches between two upright books with the same sheet of thin paper. If you lay the paper over the books, it is so flexible that it bends down and slides off the tops of the books (Fig. 13.3a). Its thickness is insufficient to

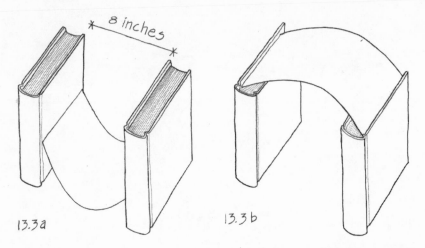

13.3a   13.3b

work as a flat plate. It lacks the needed bending stiffness to cover the span. But if we curve the paper into a cylindrical or *barrel* shape, and set it between the books, bracing its ends against the book bindings, it will become a self-standing arch, whose outward thrusts are balanced by the books, which act as buttresses (Fig. 13.3b). Similar thin arches are made of reinforced concrete in the elegant bridges of the Swiss engineer Maillart (Fig. 13.4).

If we give to the paper sheet a sharper and sharper curvature, eventually we fold it or crease it (Fig. 13.5), and the creased paper

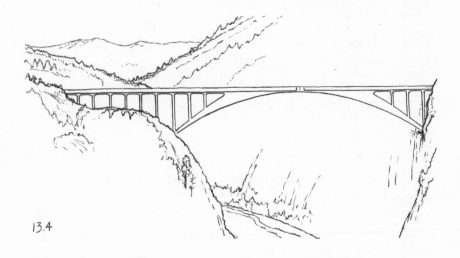

13.4

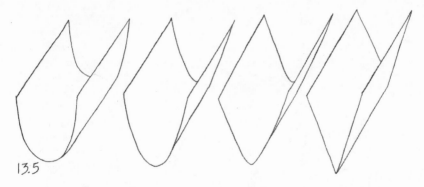

13.5

sheet acquires by this procedure great stiffness and strength. If you fold a sheet of paper lengthwise up and down every inch or so, it becomes what is called a *folded plate* (Fig. 13.6). While the flat sheet of paper could not span 8 inches between two books, the folded paper or plate can span the entire length of 11 inches and can carry additional small loads like a small book (Fig. 13.7). Since the thickness of the paper is one hundredth of an inch (or less), the span of the folded plate is 11 inches divided by one hundredth, that is, multiplied by 100, or 1,100 times its thickness! A flat, unfolded plate capable of spanning 11 inches would have to be about ½ inch thick, or 50 times thicker than the folded plate. Folded plates of reinforced concrete are used as roofs of large

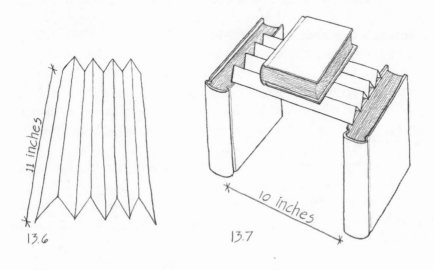

11 inches

13.6

10 inches

13.7

13.8

halls, hangars and factories, with spans of 100 feet or more (Fig. 13.8).

To make the folded plate even stiffer, you may glue to its top and bottom two flat sheets of paper (Fig. 13.9). This *sandwich plate* acts as a series of I-beams in two directions, with the folded plate as web and the flat sheets as flanges. Because of their light weight and great stiffness, sandwich plates with webs of paper and flanges of cardboard, plywood, plastics or steel are used in airplane construction, where weight is always at a premium. In such sandwich plates the web or *core* is usually made of paper honeycomb instead of simple folded paper (Fig. 13.10).

Combining the two principles of strength through curvature and strength through creasing, you can build a model arch bridge with a folded plate roadway in which the loads are supported in part by the arch and in part by the folded plate (Fig. 13.11). It is amazing to realize what a load of books such a flimsy-looking struc-

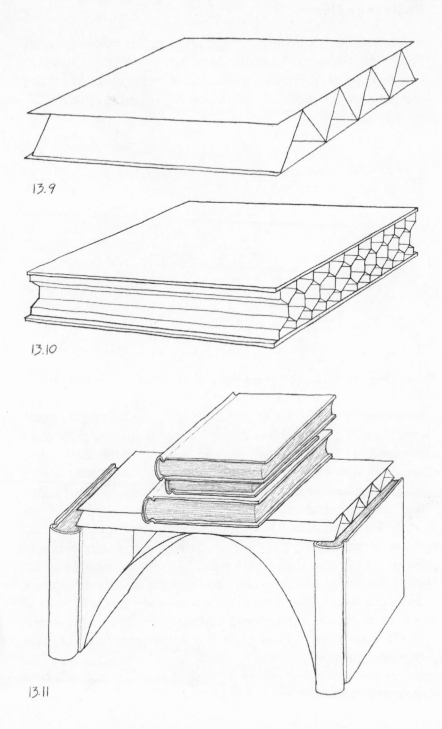

13.9

13.10

13.11

ture can support, particularly if the barrel arch is made of slightly thicker drafting paper. Actually, a full-size paper bridge has been designed by Lev Zetlin Associates as an advertising stunt for a paper company, strong enough to be crossed by a real car (Fig. 13.12).

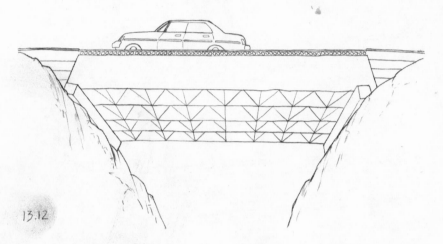

13.12

One can make the same sheet of paper even stronger by giving it a general arch curvature *and* by creasing it. Figure 13.13a shows how to do this. Draw the solid and dotted lines of this figure on a sheet of drafting paper, according to the dimensions given in the figure. Fold the sheet of drafting paper *up* along all the solid lines and then fold it *down* along the dotted lines, using a steel ruler as a guide. To make a strong structure, the folds must follow the lines very *accurately* and this will take, at first, care and patience. Each fold should be sharply creased with your nails. Starting at one of the long edges of the sheet, gather the folds together, as in Figure 13.13b, and then repeat along the opposite edge. In so doing, make sure that each crease is up along the solid lines and down along the dotted lines. Take your time in doing this, and you will end up by having creased and flattened the sheet as in Figure 13.13c. Cut its boundaries along the dotted lines so as to make them horizontal.

If you now open your accordion-like structure, you will have the *creased barrel* of Figure 13.13d.

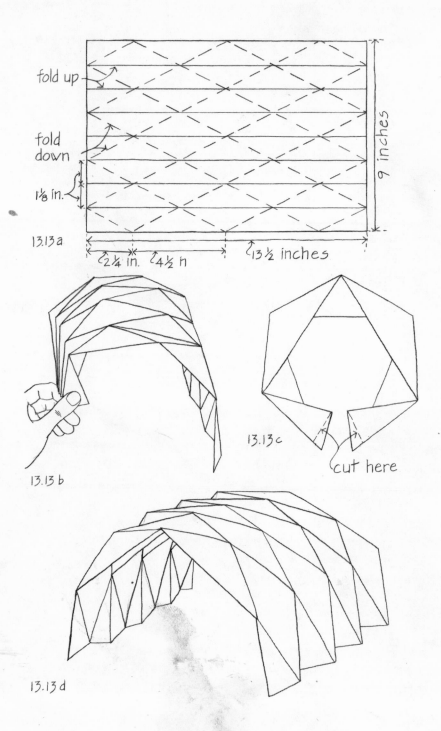

fold up

fold

down

1⅛ in.

9 inches

13.13 a

2¼ in. 4½ in 13½ inches

13.13 b

13.13 c

cut here

13.13 d

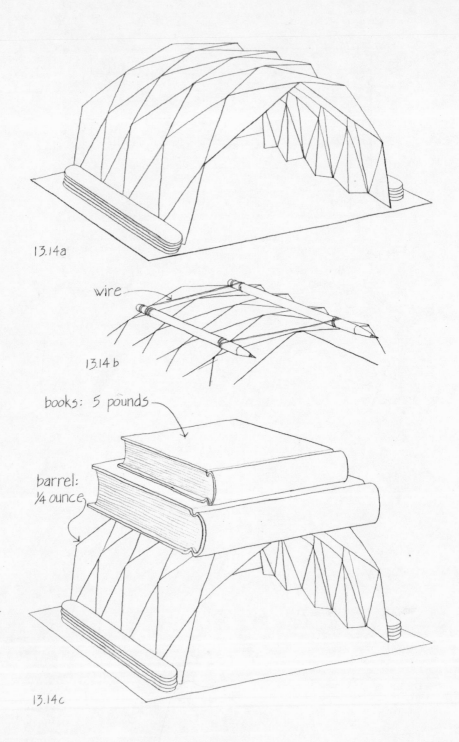

13.14a

wire

13.14 b

books: 5 pounds

barrel: ¼ ounce

13.14c

The efficiency of a structure is often measured by the ratio of the load it can carry to its own dead load. You can easily determine such ratio for the creased-paper barrel. Since a barrel, like an arch, has a tendency to thrust out, set the barrel between two wooden "buttresses" glued to a piece of cardboard (Fig. 13.14a). (The "buttresses" can be built up with tongue depressors glued one on top of the other.) Weigh the creased barrel on a postal scale. (Actually the weight of the barrel is so small that it is easier on a postal scale to measure the weight of 10 sheets of paper and divide this by 10 to obtain the weight of one sheet.) By means of two pencils and some wire, build the loading platform structure of Figure 13.14b, with the pencils a distance apart about one third of the barrel's span. You can now load the barrel with small books or other loads (Fig. 13.14c) and then weigh the platform with its book loads. You will find that a well-creased barrel can support a load of up to 300 times its own weight! Figure 13.15 shows the church of the Jesuit University in San Salvador (the capital of El Salvador, in Central America), whose reinforced concrete structure is built according to this principle and spans 100 feet. There are very few structures with such an incredible carrying capacity.

It all goes to show that giving a structure an efficient shape may be far more important than increasing the amount of its material.

13.15

14

Barrels, Dishes, Butterflies, Bicycle Wheels and Eggs

THE SIMPLE FACT THAT CURVATURE GIVES STIFFNESS AND STRENGTH to thin sheets of material has made possible a whole family of curved roofs in exciting shapes and of economical design that are called *thin shells* or *membrane roofs*.

A membrane is a sheet of material so thin that it is practically incapable of carrying loads by bending. It is usually made out of concrete, steel or wood, and can carry very heavy loads only because of its curved shape. The simplest example of such a structure is the *barrel roof*, which consists of a curved semi-cylindrical membrane (Fig. 14.1), supported along its circular boundaries rather than along its long sides. Such roofs are often used to cover factories. Although they *look* like long arches, they do not *behave* like arches, because they do not exert an outward thrust. Barrels act instead as beams supported at their ends, with a semicircular cross-section. A barrel-roof model of paper can be built by glueing the paper barrel to two vertical pieces of cardboard, as shown in Figure 14.2. The fact that the model stands up without buttresses along its sides shows that no thrust is developed there. The barrel has, like a beam,

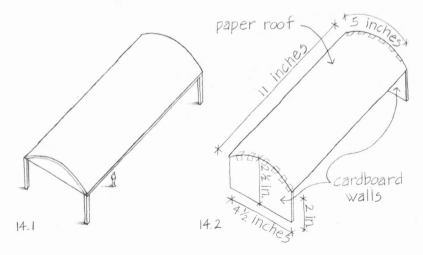

paper roof

5 inches

11 inches

cardboard walls

2½ in.

4½ inches

2 in.

14.1

14.2

compression at the top, tension at the bottom and a neutral axis. A comparison with the paper arch supported along its sides that develops a thrust (Fig. 13.3b), shows that the same geometrical shape will act in different structural ways depending on how it is supported.

A shape similar to the barrel can be formed by giving curvature to only one edge of a membrane and keeping the opposite edge straight. This type of roof is called a *conoid* and has an ideal shape for cantilevered roofs covering the stands of stadiums with either a curvature up or a curvature down (Fig. 13.2). A series of short conoids with downward curvature (Fig. 14.3a) supported on stiff frames produces a roof that allows illumination through glass panes set between adjacent conoids at the curved front of each conoid. If the conoids face the north, they get the best natural light, which is often important in factories.

When barrels and conoids are made of reinforced concrete, they require wooden *forms* on which to set the reinforcing steel and pour the concrete (Fig. 14.3b). The initial cost of making the formwork is usually high, but it can be reduced by pouring many shells on the same form and lifting the shells on top of their supporting columns after the concrete sets, in 3 to 7 days.

To avoid the cost of the formwork, roofs in the shape of

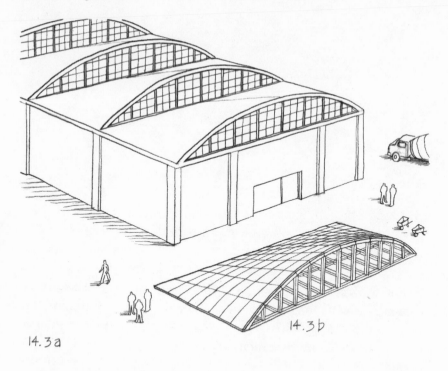

14.3a   14.3b

dishes have been built very economically of concrete slabs and steel cables by the following procedure. A reinforced concrete ring is first poured on top of a circular wall (or a series of columns set in a circle) and steel radial cables are strung from the outer concrete ring to an inner smaller steel ring set about one-tenth of the span lower than the outer concrete ring and temporarily supported on a scaffold (Fig. 14.4a). A series of prefabricated, pie-shaped concrete slabs is then set on the radial cables (Fig. 14.4b) and loaded with sandbags or bricks, thus stretching the cables even more than they are stretched by the weight of the slabs. After that, the radial and circular joints between the slabs are filled with mortar (a mixture of water, cement and sand). When the mortar gets hard, the roof becomes one single piece of concrete. At this point, the sandbags or bricks are removed. Though the cables, free of the extra burden of the sandbags or bricks, tend to shorten, they cannot do so, because they are gripped by the hardened mortar, so they main-

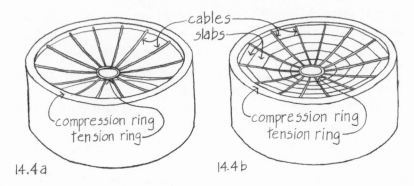

14.4a   14.4b

tain their tension. The final result is a dish-shaped roof, with upward curvatures, built without the use of formwork, and very rigid.

The first roof of this kind, built by the Uruguayan engineer
Leonel Viera, covered a round stadium 310 feet across with slabs
only 2 inches thick. (They could be made this thin because they
only span a few feet, from cable to cable.) The roof of Madison
Square Garden in New York City, also 310 feet across (Fig. 14.5), is
built on the same principle.

One of the problems presented by dish roofs is that rainwater
or snow can accumulate on their upward-curved, or concave, shape
and produce large loads on the dish. To avoid this danger the water
is pumped through pipes over the rim of the dish by electric
pumps located at the center of the roof as soon as the water's

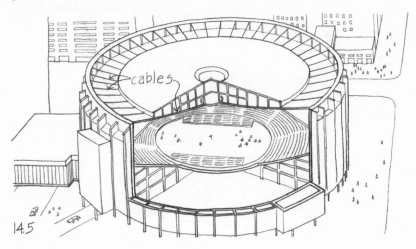

14.5

depth is more than one or two inches. Snow and ice are melted into water by electric heat and then pumped out. (A gas generator activates the pump if the electric current goes off in a storm.)

If you remember how vertical loads develop tension in upward-curved cables and compression in downward-curved arches, you will realize that the tension in the radial cables of a dish roof develops compression in the outer concrete ring and tension in the inner steel ring, since the cable tension acts *toward* the center of the outer ring and *away* from the center of the inner ring (Fig. 14.6). This is why the outer ring is usually made of inexpensive concrete, which stands compression well, and the inner ring of steel, which is strong in tension.

Recently, Russian engineers have greatly improved the design of dish roofs. They have built roofs in the shape of ellipses and have even used steel sheet instead of concrete panels for their surfaces.

To avoid the rain problem, roofs have been built with one outer compression ring and two inner tension rings, one set above and one below the outer ring. Two sets of tensed radial cables, kept separate by *spreaders*, connect the two inner rings to the outer ring (Fig. 14.7). Such roofs are called *bicycle-wheel roofs*, for obvious reasons. Their cables act like the spokes of a bicycle wheel, the outer compressed ring as its rim and the two inner rings as its hub. A bicycle wheel is a stiff, light, vertical wheel and a bicycle-wheel roof is nothing else but a gigantic horizontal bicycle wheel. In all

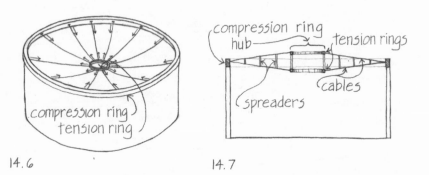

compression ring
tension ring

compression ring
hub — tension rings
cables
spreaders

14.6   14.7

cases, the roofing material of bicycle-wheel roofs is set on top of the upper set of cables, so that the rainwater runs off by itself over the roof rim. The snow slides off these roofs as the heat inside the building melts the snow layer in contact with the roof.

Domes have been built for centuries to cover majestically large areas, using concrete, brick and, more recently, steel. The Pantheon in Rome was originally built with a dome of bricks and concrete in 27 B.C. as a temple to all the Roman gods. It spans 143 feet (Fig. 14.8). It is now a church, in which the bodies of the last Italian kings are buried. The dome of the church of Hagia Sophia in Istanbul, Turkey, was built between 532 A.D. and 537 A.D. by the Byzantine emperor Justinian, of large, flat bricks and spans 107 feet (Fig. 14.9). It became a mosque under the Turkish domination and is now a museum. The dome of St. Peter's in Rome, the largest church of the Christian world, consists of a double dome, one inside the other, spanning 137 feet. Between the walls of the domes are located stairs by which to climb to the top (Fig. 14.10). It was originally designed by Michelangelo, the famous sculptor and painter, who sculpted the statue of the *Pietà* in the same church and painted the frescoes of the Sistine Chapel. The most famous dome of the Renaissance is that of Santa Maria del Fiore in Florence, designed and built by Brunelleschi between 1420 A.D. and 1434 A.D. with the help of a simple scaffold, as a double octagonal dome of brick spanning 138 feet (Fig. 14.11).

The largest concrete dome in the world today is the double dome of the C.N.I.T. Exhibition Hall in Paris, built in 1958, spanning 676 feet and supported on three points (Fig. 14.12). The largest steel dome to date is the dome of the Louisiana Superdome in New Orleans, built in 1975, spanning 680 feet and ribbed with a complex cage of steel beams (Fig. 14.13). These are among the largest unencumbered spaces covered by man at a time when our culture demands that as many as 60,000 to 80,000 people gather under the same roof to participate in a sports event or to attend a religious ceremony.

How does a dome work? If the *compressive* arch may be

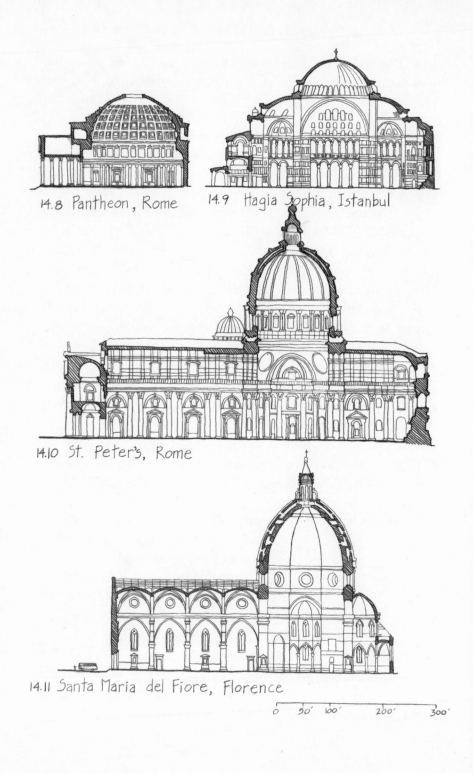

14.8 Pantheon, Rome

14.9 Hagia Sophia, Istanbul

14.10 St. Peter's, Rome

14.11 Santa Maria del Fiore, Florence

0   50′ 100′   200′   300′

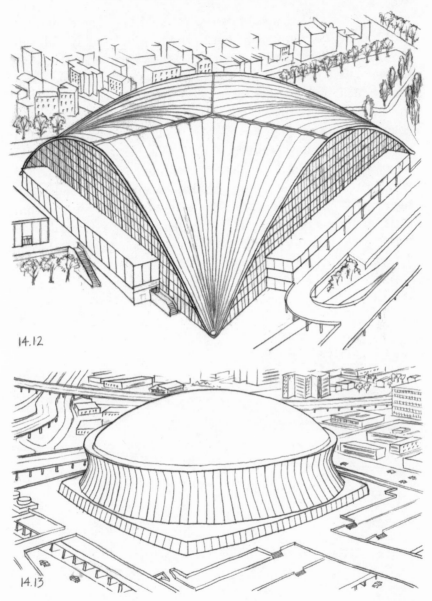

14.12

14.13

thought of as the opposite of the *tensile* cable, the dome could be called the opposite of the dish. Whatever its material, a dome consists of a series of arches set around a vertical axis, whose outward thrusts are absorbed by a main bottom ring, but also by rings at various levels all the way to its top (Fig. 14.14). These rings prevent the arches from moving out to the sides or laterally and, with their great stiffness, they support the arches. Because of the lateral support given by the rings or *parallels*, the arches, or *meridians*, can be made much lighter than isolated arches, without reducing the dome stiffness. In a reinforced concrete dome the reinforced concrete arches are built one next to the other, creating a continuous surface with downward curvatures. The rings consist of circular hoops of concrete with reinforcing bars hidden in the concrete. A peculiarity of domes in the shape of half-spheres is that, under load, their meridional arches tend to move inward at the top and compress the top parallel rings, while they tend to move outward at the bottom and put into tension the bottom parallels (Fig. 14.15). Thus the area of the dome near its bottom (actually below an angle of 52° from its vertical axis) must be well reinforced in tension, as is done with the steel hoop of a wine barrel (Fig. 14.16), while

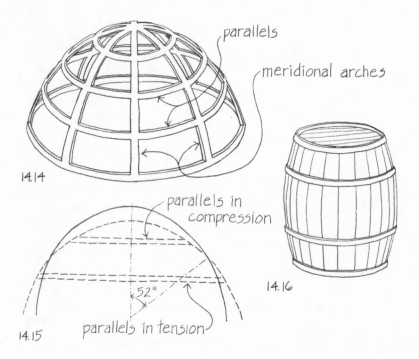

parallels

meridional arches

14.14

parallels in compression

parallels in tension

52°

14.15

14.16

in the area near the top the compression in the parallels can be taken by the concrete of the dome itself.

You can easily appreciate the cause of the dome stiffness by realizing that in order to try to flatten half a rubber ball, you must deform it by stretching it or by introducing cuts along its meridians (Fig. 14.17). (On the other hand, a barrel can be flattened without any effort since it becomes flat by itself unless it is buttressed [Fig. 14.18].) Few people would guess that a reinforced concrete dome in the shape of half a sphere with a diameter or span of 100 feet and a thickness of only 4 inches, deflects at its top, under its own dead load and a heavy snow load, less than one-tenth of an inch! In this dome, the diameter is 100 times 12 inches or 1,200 inches which is 300 times the thickness of 4 inches. The span of 1,200 inches is 1,200 divided by 0.1 inches or 12,000 times its top's deflection. As a comparison, the span of a beam (whatever its material) is about 20 times its thickness or depth and about 360

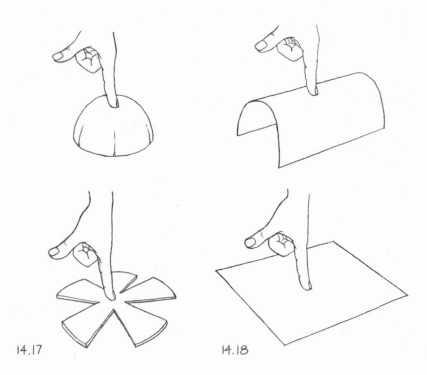

14.17   14.18

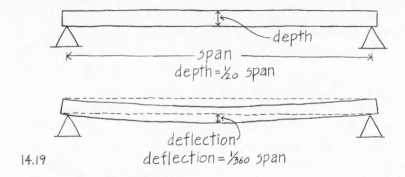

14.19

depth = ½₀ span

deflection = ½₃₆₀ span

times its deflection (Fig. 14.19). Thin domes are almost incredibly strong and stiff. Their thickness is only limited by the danger of buckling, which is always present when a thin structural element is compressed. Their only other disadvantage is the high cost of their curved formwork.

You may be curious to know whether the best known natural "dome," the shell of an egg, is structurally efficient. It may be disappointing to find that because the egg shell is made of a brittle material (to allow the chicks to break it and come out), it has a span only 30 times its thickness. An egg shell is quite thick, but it is also quite strong. If you set 4 uncooked eggs in 4 egg cups, surrounding them first with a padding of cotton to give them good contact with the cups, put 4 more upside down, padded egg cups on top of the eggs and support a plank of wood on them, you may astonish an audience by standing on the plank without breaking the eggs (Fig. 14.20). (The audience will usually be delighted if at the end of the performance you break the eggs in a bowl as if you were ready to scramble them.)

Barrels, dishes and domes have curvatures either upward or downward *in all directions* (Fig. 14.21a). (The barrels have one direction that is not curved. It is parallel to their axis, which is straight [Fig. 14.21b].)

The last surfaces we wish to mention in this chapter have curvatures *up* in certain directions and *down* in others (Fig. 14.21c). They look like, and are called, *saddle surfaces*.

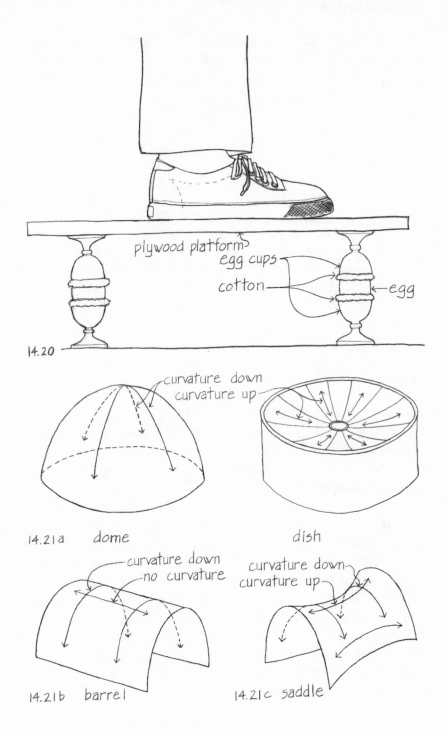

plywood platform

egg cups

cotton

egg

14.20

curvature down
curvature up

14.21a dome

dish

curvature down
no curvature

14.21b barrel

curvature down
curvature up

14.21c saddle

You can obtain one such surface by pulling up on two opposite corners of a handkerchief and pulling down on the other two opposite corners (Fig. 14.22). To understand that a saddle surface

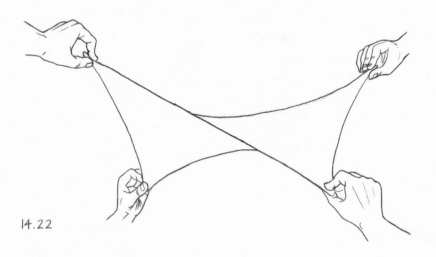

14.22

(called a *hyperbolic paraboloid*; the British abbreviate this to the simpler word *hypar*) can be defined by straight lines only, you can build a model of it by means of tongue depressors and string as shown in Figure 14.23. The frame for a hypar (see Fig. 14.23a) is a square with one corner D above the plane of the other three corners A, B and C.

To build it, staple together with a regular stapler two tongue depressors at right angles to each other and two more also at right angles (Fig. 14.23b). Hold in your left hand the ends B of one depressor of each right angle assembly and rotate one assembly with respect to the other about B until the other free ends cross and extend about one inch over the other at D (Fig. 14.23c). Staple in this position the two ends B you hold in your hand (Fig. 14.23c). Now push the sticking-out ends together (in so doing, the corner D will lift from the plane of the corners A, B and C) and staple them together (Fig. 14.23d). This last operation requires that the de-

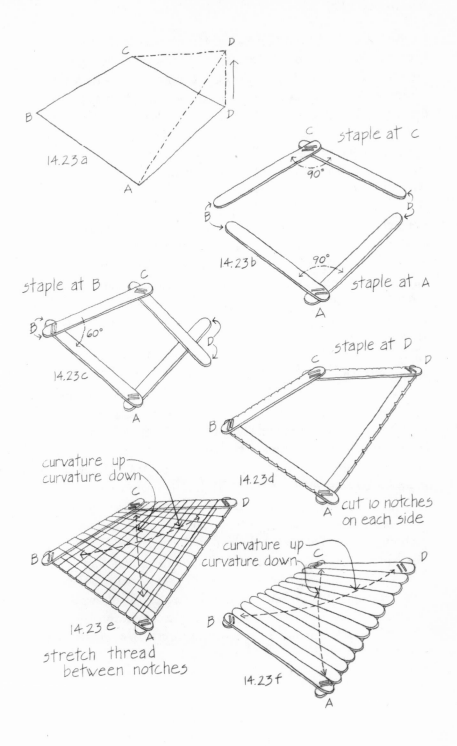

14.23 a

staple at c

90°

14.23 b

90°

staple at A

staple at B

60°

14.23 c

staple at D

14.23 d

cut 10 notches
on each side

curvature up
curvature down

14.23 e

stretch thread
between notches

curvature up
curvature down

14.23 f

pressors be twisted a bit. With a nail file or a small jig saw cut evenly spaced notches (try 8 notches) along the outer edges of all 4 depressors. Pull a thread, fixed in the first notch of one depressor by a knot, *over* the depressor, across to the first notch of the opposite depressor, then under and along the depressor to its second notch, and up and across to the second notch of the first depressor. Continue as shown in Fig. 14.23e until you have gone through all the notches of two opposite depressors and then continue across the other two depressors to make a square web. Although the strings of the square web are straight, since they are in tension, they define a curved surface with curvature down along the diagonal A-C and with curvature up along the other diagonal B-D (Fig. 14.23e).

Instead of threading a thread from notch to notch, you may staple to two opposite sides of the hypar frame tongue depressors parallel to the other two sides, by twisting them a bit. You will thus obtain the actual full surface of the hypar (Fig. 14.23f), rather than the square web.

A hypar roof covering a square area can be obtained by supporting the corners A and C on two columns so that the corners B and D stick up (Fig. 14.24). It looks like a soaring bird or a butterfly. Since the curvature along A-C is downward and it is also downward in vertical planes parallel to A-C, the hypar works as a series of arches parallel to each other in the direction A-C, pulled by a series of "cables" with curvature up in the direction B-D. Lovely hypars of reinforced concrete are among the most efficient roofs ever built. They can be quite thin, as buckling of the compressed arches is prevented by the supporting tensed "cables," which are actually reinforcing bars parallel to B-D hidden in the concrete. Figure 14.25a shows how four hypar units, of the type described, can be connected by struts along their inclined edges to obtain large hypar umbrellas supported on one column. Figure 14.25b shows a *hypar roof* made of four upside-down units connected along their horizontal edges with tie-rods to absorb the thrusts of their triangular truss edges and supported on four columns.

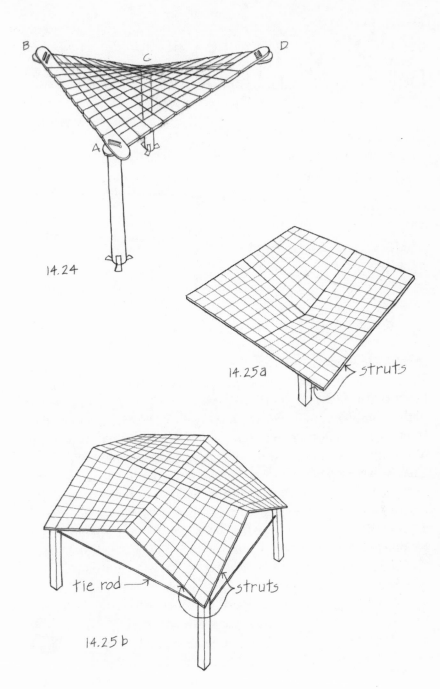

B

D

C

A

14.24

14.25a ← struts

tie rod → ↙struts

14.25b

15

Balloons ... and Back to the Tent

IF YOU BLOW UP A SAUSAGE-SHAPED BALLOON, IT BECOMES STIFF. The internal air pressure acts against the wall of the balloon in all directions so that its cylindrical shape becomes longer and is tensed both lengthwise and crosswise (Fig. 15.1). (Remember that lengthening is always due to tension.) The balloon will be capable of acting as a column and of supporting a certain amount of load. This is because the load tends to compress its longitudinal walls, but these, thin as they are, will not buckle and collapse until the compression due to the load cancels the tension due to the internal air pressure. You can prove this by putting a cup on top of the balloon and loading it with a number of small books or a small glass that you gradually fill with water (Fig. 15.2).

It is just as easy to prove that the inflated balloon can act as a beam. If you hold it in one hand, it can cantilever under its own light weight, but it can also support a load hanging from a string ring at its tip (Fig. 15.3a). The tip load, through beam action (see Ch. 3), will introduce an additional tension in the upper part of the cantilever, but will compress the lower part of the balloon.

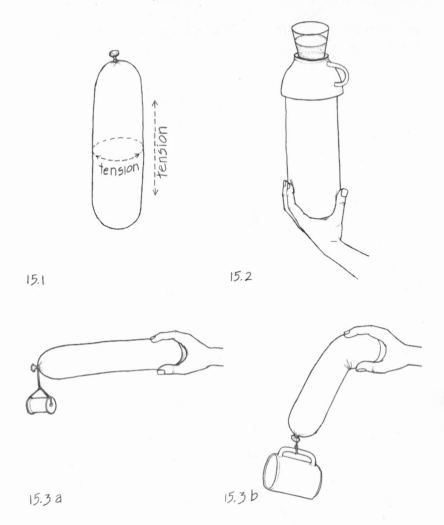

15.1

15.2

15.3 a

15.3 b

Until the load becomes large enough to cancel out the inflation tension through beam compression in the lower part of the balloon, the balloon will cantilever. When the beam compression becomes higher than the inflation tension, the balloon buckles on the underside next to your hand (Fig. 15.3b) and collapses.

By the same mechanism, the inflated balloon can carry a midspan load as a simply supported beam if you balance it on two books standing upright. It will collapse only if the compression at its center top, due to the weight of the load, cancels out the inflation tension (Fig. 15.4a, b).

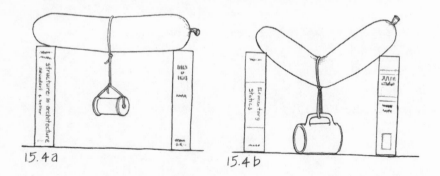

15.4 a

15.4 b

Frames (Fig. 15.5a) and even trusses (Fig. 15.5b) can be built using inflated balloons. These are extremely light and carry loads hundreds of times their own weight as you have seen. If you have a friend working at a supermarket, you may be allowed to use one

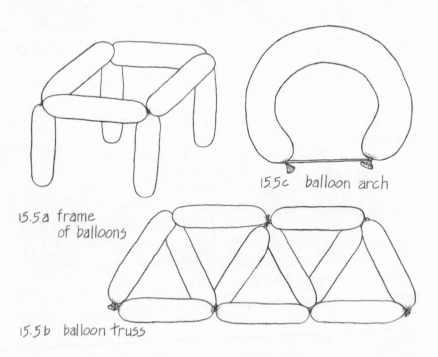

15.5c balloon arch

15.5a frame of balloons

15.5b balloon truss

of their bag sealers that close bags tight with red adhesive tape. They work very well on inflated balloons too, provided you first tie a knot at the end of the balloon and then put it through the bag sealer. This makes your experiment easier.

Going one step further, you can bend a balloon into an arch shape by tying its ends with a string (Fig. 15.5c). A number of these arches can then be joined together, one next to the other, by weaving three or more strings above and below the arches, to build a barrel. Figure 15.6 shows one such *pneumatic barrel* used to build

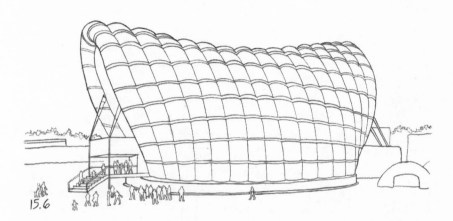

15.6

the Fuji Pavilion at the Osaka, Japan, World's Fair of 1970. The walls of its balloons were made of a strong plastic fabric and the barrel, spanning 164 feet, was so stiffened by the internal pressure of air that it could resist the lateral forces of strong winds.

Inflatable balloons are also used as inexpensive formwork on which to pour reinforced concrete shells. Once the concrete sets, an opening is cut in the shell, the air is let out, and the balloon is pulled out through the opening. It can then be used as many as a hundred more times to build other shells such as the one shown in Fig. 15.7. Such shells are called Bini-shells from the name of their Italian inventor, Dante Bini, and can span up to 300 feet.

Now that such strong plastic fabrics, made out of nylon, for

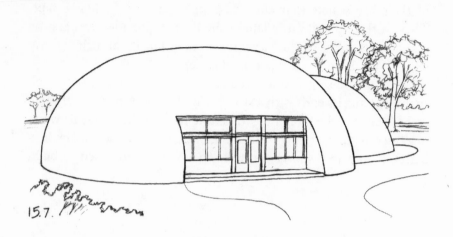

15.7.

example, can be cheaply bought, a variety of air structures can be economically built. A lens-type pneumatic roof is made by glueing together two round sheets of nylon all along their edges to form a flat balloon. It is then inflated and supported on a ring of steel on columns. Figure 15.8a shows the roof and frame of one such structure for the MEBAC Theater in Cambridge, Massachusetts, that spans 150 feet and covers 2,000 seats. The sides of the theater look like a tent (Fig. 15.8b) and the entire structure can be dismantled in half an hour in case of hurricanes.

You can build a model of such a double-wall pneumatic roof by glueing or Scotch taping shut the open side of a supermarket

15.8a

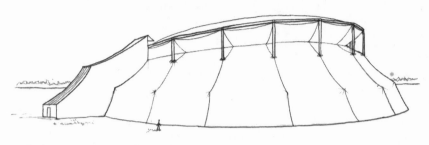

15.8b

plastic bag, but leaving a small opening at one corner through which to blow it up. It can then be hung by its four corners on paper I-beams mounted on heavy cardboard, after closing the opening with Scotch tape (Fig. 15.9).

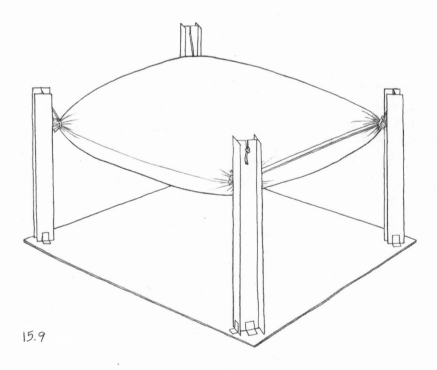

15.9

The most impressive use of pneumatic membranes, as the inflated plastic fabrics are called, is in covering large areas such as
tennis courts (Fig. 15.10) or sport stadiums. In this latter case

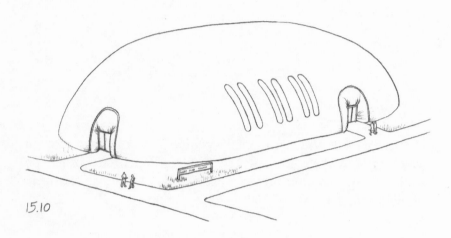

15.10

only one sheet of fabric is used, shaped like a somewhat flattened
dome. It is supported on a vertical wall or an inclined buttress or
berm and anchored air-tight to the berm around its boundary. It
is blown up by electric fans through holes in the wall or berm
and kept up by pumping into it a small amount of air to com-
pensate for the air lost through door openings and through the
fabric itself. When the dimensions of these roofs reach hundreds
of feet, it is necessary to reinforce the fabric with steel cables set
above or attached below it in a network and tensed by the inflated
fabric. The fabric then needs only to be strong enough to span
the small distance from cable to cable, as in the Pontiac Stadium
roof by David Geiger (Fig. 15.11).

You can make a model of such a pneumatic roof (Fig. 15.12a)
by following these instructions:

    a. Drill a hole about ¼ of an inch in diameter at the center
       of a 2 ft. by 3 ft. piece of plywood and insert in it a bicycle

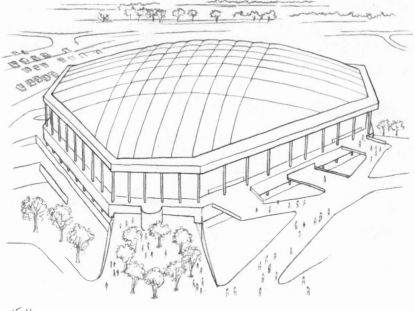

15.11

tire valve. Use Duco or similar cement to stick the valve in the hole.

b. Buy in a medical supply store a thin rubber sheet, 2 ft. by 3 ft., and attach it to the plywood by means of closely spaced thumb tacks all around the edge, after turning the edge under, thus doubling it. Tape a strong adhesive tape over the thumb tacks all around the boundary (Fig. 15.12b).

c. Attach to the plywood across the 2 ft. width of the rubber sheet 6 pieces of string about 2 ft. 4 in. long, spaced about 5 inches from one another (Fig. 15.12a).

d. Inflate the rubber sheet through the valve in the plywood by means of bicycle pump, until the string becomes taut (Fig. 15.12a). (The strings make the model stiffer by allowing a higher air pressure to be used without bursting the

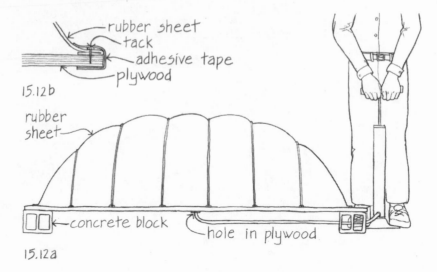

rubber sheet
tack
adhesive tape
plywood

15.12b

rubber sheet→

concrete block

hole in plywood

15.12a

rubber sheet. They act like the steel cables in a pneumatic roof.)

e. Experiment with strings in different directions, using as a model, for example, the network of the Pontiac Stadium roof.

Since pneumatic roofs can cover hundreds of acres and are made of fabrics that cannot burn, they could be used to cover entire shopping centers and even small towns. Such roofs are actually supported by columns of air, certainly the cheapest of all structural materials. It is hard to imagine any other structural system that could cover such large areas without intermediate supports.

The availability of strong plastic fabrics and of steel cables has made possible the construction of the modern tent. This is a far cry from the skin-and-pole tent of our ancestors and even from the large circus tents of a few years ago.

Large modern tents (not the kind used for outdoor camping) are built by shaping into the most varied and imaginative forms sheets of plastic fabrics by using a net of steel cables, supported on masts or hanging from walls. They have barrel, dome and saddle shapes, and are used as permanent roofs of large sport installations

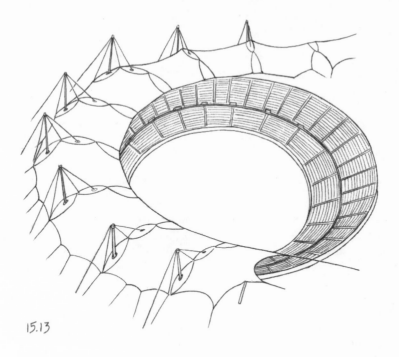

15.13

and other wide areas. The permanent tent over the stands of the Munich Stadium, designed by Frei Otto in 1972 in Germany, covers 20 acres (Fig. 15.13). By using the principle of the spider-web, man has thus been able to cover large areas with the lightest of structures.

Human inventiveness, with the help of modern technology, has created structures of great beauty and of sizes undreamed of in the past. There is no limit to the achievements of the future in this fascinating field of human activity, in which the art of architecture and the science of engineering work together to improve the way in which man lives.

Index